Better Homes and Gardens

KITCHEN

Planning & Decorating

This cheerful kitchen with cabinets finished with cherry stain carries out a mood of warm, country living. A large, copper hood above the slate-topped island provides ventilation and lighting for the cooking-work surface. Niches above windows display a collection of prized pottery.

BETTER HOMES AND GARDENS BOOKS
Editorial Director: Don Dooley
Managing Editor: Malcolm E. Robinson   Art Director: John Berg
Senior Editor: Marie Schulz
Copy Editor: Lawrence Clayton
Designers: Julie Zesch, Harijs Priekulis
Contributing Editor: Ruth H. Johnson

CONTENTS

INTRODUCTION

A kitchen that is both functional and attractive does not happen by accident. It is carefully planned, taking into account the physical layout of the kitchen, and the growing needs of the family. Planning is especially important, for today's kitchens cannot be rearranged easily to correct mistakes in design and organization. Many major items are built in—cabinets, counters, sink—and are expensive to replace. In order to avoid living with mistakes or making expensive adjustments, plan ahead.

The first step in planning and decorating your kitchen is to decide just what you want. Analyze your family's life-style—where do you prefer to eat family meals, how do you like to entertain, what are the ages and interests of family members, and what are your own kitchen work habits? The next step, naturally, is to figure out exactly how much money you can afford to budget for kitchen remodeling and/or decorating, and for furnishings.

Take a look at your family's eating habits. Do you like to eat family meals in or near the kitchen because you have small children and the clean-up process is quicker and easier? Or is yours a family of adults who enjoy leisurely eating in the dining room?

Do you have a wide age span in your family? Does the man of the house go to work at one time, and the children depart for school at various other times? If so, the entire family will probably not sit down to breakfast at the same time, and the homemaker will appreciate a handy snack counter where breakfast literally can be served in minutes. When it comes to the evening meals, and the entire family gathers to dine together, a dining area or dining room, or family room located nearby, would be the best choice for eating and pleasant conversation.

Next, consider your style of entertaining. Do you like to entertain small groups at formal sit-down dinners? Or do you prefer informal, buffet-type meals—or outdoor meals—when you have

guests? The type of entertaining you enjoy most should influence your choice of dining facilities and furnishings.

Family activities and interests are another factor. Do you have small children you like to keep a watchful eye on while you are performing kitchen tasks? Or do you and older family members spend your leisure time working on hobby and craft projects, reading, or listening to music? In either case, a combination kitchen-activity room is the perfect solution for you and your family.

And what about your kitchen work habits? Do you spend so much time in the kitchen that you'd like having it equally as decorative as it is functional, even though the accessories displayed on open shelves and mounted on the walls require dusting or cleaning at frequent intervals? Or do you have a job or other interests that take you away from home a great deal? Then, your prime concern is having a kitchen that is purely functional with the emphasis placed on keeping maintenance and cleaning chores at a minimum. Let these factors play a large part in determining your choice of kitchen style, equipment, and accessories.

Also, look at the number of people who will use the kitchen at one time. Are there teen-agers or others in the family or full- or part-time help to help you with kitchen chores? If so, you will need ample work space for two or more people.

Finally, decide how much you can budget for kitchen improvement. Can you pay for it in one lump sum? If not, investigate different means of financing it and the cost of each. Or plan the entire project, but do each step as your income permits.

All of the above factors should be considered whether you are planning a kitchen for a new home, a major remodeling project, or simply a minor improvement and updating of your kitchen.

chapter 1

KITCHEN PLANNING

The dividends of a well-planned kitchen are many and long-lasting, but they come only from careful thought. In planning a new kitchen or remodeling an older one, give primary consideration to the present living habits of your family, plus possible future ones. An analysis of your own likes and dislikes also is important, as is a complete list of the benefits and shortcomings of your present kitchen.

Early in the planning stage, decide how much money you can spend. Although many things are needed to remodel a kitchen, it is possible to have a well-planned kitchen at a fairly moderate cost because of the wide price range of appliances, cabinets, and materials available. Remodeling doesn't have to be done all at one time. If you're on a tight budget, plan the entire project first, and then remodel one step at a time. Do not, however, plan each step haphazardly.

There are several arrangements to fit different shapes and sizes of kitchens. If you are unsure about which arrangement will best fit your needs, seek the advice of an experienced kitchen planner.

Careful thought led to this striking one-wall kitchen. Work flows smoothly, with ample work space for two cooks, if need be. There is storage aplenty—hidden behind a wallpapered facade. High cabinets store seldom-used utensils, dinnerware, and serving items.

KITCHEN LAYOUTS

The secret to good kitchen planning is using space wisely. This involves arranging each work center so that the work of preparing and serving food and the cleaning up progresses smoothly, with a minimum of steps and the least expenditure of energy. The work centers are: the refrigerator, cooking, cleanup, and food preparation—the food preparation center generally is combined either with the refrigerator or the range. For example, time, energy, and many steps are saved when the mixing center is located between the refrigerator and sink. This is especially true if the work counters are continuous—unbroken by doorways. (See the chart on page 11 for traffic patterns.) In addition, there may be supplementary centers such as one for eating or for meal planning.

While you may want to have a kitchen that is unique, it makes better sense to follow a basic plan that has been developed for greatest efficiency. Depending upon the shape of the kitchen you wish to remodel, or the architectural design of the home you are building, use the following guides to help you plan a kitchen that will be both efficient and functional.

One-wall. This plan is also referred to as a pullman style because all the major appliances form a continuous line along one wall. It is a style that frequently is found in apartments and summer homes, or wherever floor width is limited. Since there are no corners, the arrangement eliminates difficult-to-reach storage in base and upper cabinets. If the wall is rather long, there is usually less crowding than in other styles of kitchens. Although work does not progress in a step-saving triangular pattern, the distance between work centers is usually not excessive. However, in this style of kitchen, there is very often a door at each end, resulting in through-traffic which interrupts activity. A one-wall plan is most efficient if the sink is centrally located, with the range and refrigerator at either end and work centers between the equipment. If the counter space is minimal, supplement it with a serving cart or portable dishwasher with work top.

Galley. In the galley or corridor plan, the appliances and cabinets are placed along opposite walls. It is most efficient when the sink, refrigerator, and mix centers line one wall, with cooking and serving areas opposite. This arrangement adapts easily to an open kitchen-family room when one of the work walls is open above the base cabinets, forming a divider between the two areas. If the counters are not spread too far apart, the triangular work pattern is compact and efficient. However, if there is a doorway at each end, there will be a traffic problem.

L-shape. Here, the appliances and work counters are placed along two adjacent walls. The arrangement provides for a smooth sequence between the activity centers so that work is less likely to be interrupted by unwanted traffic. The shape of the kitchen permits flexibility in location of appliances, storage, and counters.

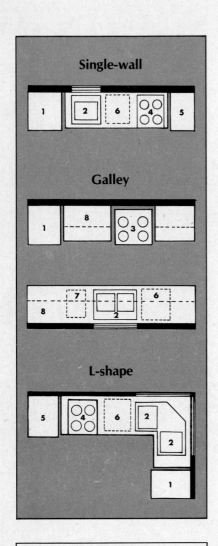

Single-wall

Galley

L-shape

1. *Refrigerator*
2. *Sink*
3. *Freestanding range*
4. *Built-in cook top*
5. *Built-in wall oven*
6. *Dishwasher*
7. *Trash compactor*
8. *Overhead wall cabinets*

The work flow should progress from the refrigerator to sink, to cooking and serving; any other sequence of activity centers causes backtracking and reduces efficiency. This plan is well suited to kitchen-family room arrangements. The short leg of the L can be a range-serving center, with an extended counter to serve for informal dining. To do this, extend the counter depth and raise it to a snack bar height, or lower the extension so it will accommodate standard-height dining chairs. If it is designed with care, this style of kitchen can accommodate two cooks conveniently.

U-shape. This plan requires a larger floor area than the previous styles—eight feet is the minimum recommended for both lengthwise and crosswise dimensions. However, it is considered tops in efficiency. The work centers can be arranged in good sequence with minimum distances between. Customarily, the sink is at the base of the U, with the refrigerator and range flanking the sidewalls opposite each other. There is a minimum of wasted steps and motion if the appliances form the points of an equal-legged triangle. Work flow is not interrupted by traffic, and counters are continuous and provide ample work space. The U-shape plan permits ample wall cabinets and window area. It can also be readily adapted to open kitchen-family rooms. If the U is too small, however, it is not comfortable for more than one cook.

Kitchen with an island. If space is not a problem, add an island to the kitchen. Customarily, an island is situated in the central portion of a large kitchen and is open all-around. The beauty of this type of arrangement is that it brings work centers closer together, reducing the number of steps between them. It is an ideal solution for making a large, older kitchen more efficient. Different variations of islands are described on pages 97-98.

Kitchen with a peninsula. Larger kitchens may incorporate a peninsula to put otherwise wasted space to good use. A peninsula is essentially an extension (in open floor area) of a work counter or row of cabinets. It generally serves as a divider between two areas, simultaneously providing additional counter and storage space. For more about types of peninsulas, see pages 96-97.

MEASURING FOR KITCHEN PLANNING

In order to determine which plan on these two pages might work best for you, you'll need some accurate measurements. If you are building a new home or adding to your present one, you can work with the architect's or contractor's prints. Otherwise, you'll need to make your own sketch. Here's how to do it. To draw the outline of your kitchen, take measurements at the counter height. Indicate the location of windows, doors (and how they swing), plumbing, light switches, fans, and registers. Note any structural irregularities such as closets, chimneys, ducts, or radiators. When the outline is completed, experiment with more than one arrangement, checking the work centers, and the work and traffic patterns. Study each one carefully in order to determine which one best fits the available space and your working requirements.

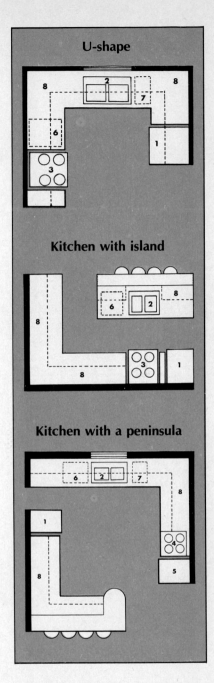

U-shape

Kitchen with island

Kitchen with a peninsula

1. *Refrigerator*
2. *Sink*
3. *Freestanding range*
4. *Built-in cook top*
5. *Built-in wall oven*
6. *Dishwasher*
7. *Trash compactor*
8. *Overhead wall cabinets*

PLANNING SPACE

A well-designed kitchen, in addition to having an efficient floor plan, has sufficient work space, counters, and cabinets at a height comfortable for the homemaker. When too much space is allotted, efficiency is greatly reduced; if space is at a bare minimum, convenience suffers. Adequate clearance between facing appliances or work counters is also important. Too much space results in unnecessary steps between the areas; too little causes traffic problems and interruption of meal preparation and cleanup.

Cabinets. Factory-built base cabinets are made in 3-inch modules from 9 to 48 inches wide with wall cabinets, 12 to 33 inches. Try to provide at least 10 or more linear feet of base cabinets in addition to corner ones. Have adjustable shelves for flexibility and for maximum use of space, especially in small kitchens.

Working heights. Ideally, the work surface height should be tailored to the height of the homemaker. This is possible with custom-built cabinets. However, deviating too much from the standard height could limit resale of a home. The usual counter surface is 36 inches from the floor. Since it is less tiring to do some kitchen tasks—mixing, chopping, or rolling out pastry—on a surface that is 6 to 7 inches below elbow height, it may be desirable to provide one counter that is lower than standard. Some manufacturers do build a lower unit, 32 to 33 inches high.

Space requirements for work centers. Listed below are recommended cabinet and working space requirements for carrying out the various duties connected with meal preparation and serving. Bear in mind that a counter may serve more than one center. If this is the case, take the figures given for the two counters that will share the space, and add 12 inches to the larger figure. For example, if the refrigerator and mix center are combined, a space of 48 to 54 inches (12 plus 36 to 42 inches) would be advisable.

Center	Recommended Counter Space
Refrigerator	15 to 18 inches on latch side of door.
Sink-cleanup	24 to 30 inches to right of sink, 18 to 30 to the left.
Mixing	36 to 42 inches.
Range or built-in cooking surface	15 to 24 inches of heatproof material. Plan 15 to 18 inches adjacent to built-in oven.

Clearance. For appliances that are placed opposite one another, a clearance of 5 to 6 feet is suggested. This distance also permits two to work without interfering with each other as they move back and forth. A clearance of 15 inches between counter and wall cabinets is needed for small appliances such as a coffee maker, blender, and mixer. For standard depth cabinets over a sink, allow 24 inches above the sink rim; between a range top and upper cabinet, plan 27 to 36 inches, depending upon local code.

1. *Pullout counter height, 30"*
2. *Mixing counter height, 32"*
3. *Standard counter height, 36"*
4. *Switches and outlets, 44"*
5. *To bottom of wall cabinet, 55"*
6. *To top of wall cabinet, 87"*
7. *Average ceiling height, 96"*
8. *Depth of wall cabinet, 13"*
9. *Depth of base cabinet, 24"*
10. *Depth minus toe space, 21"*

BASIC KITCHEN REQUIREMENTS

Other aspects of kitchen planning that require careful consideration include the location and the basic structure of the kitchen.
If you are building a new home, or doing extensive remodeling of
an older one, you should think about the actual location of the
kitchen in relation to other rooms in the home. If you are remodeling within existing framework, you will want to be certain that
the basic structure is sound and that pipes and ductwork are in
good condition. Also, be sure that wiring, lighting, and ventilation are ample to meet present or possible future needs.

Location. If you have a choice, consideration should be given
to the location of the kitchen in relation to where food may be
served—daily meals, more formal ones, and outdoor patio or deck
meals. Plan the location so that it is accessible from the garage or
carport, for convenient grocery delivery. Preferably, the kitchen
should be out of view from the front entrance and formal living
room. If there are youngsters in the family, it is desirable to have
the play area within range of vision. Try to plan the placement of
the doors so that the traffic bypasses the major work center areas
within the kitchen while meals are being prepared.

Basic structure. In remodeling a kitchen, begin literally from
the ground up. Check for a firm foundation, and repair any flaws
in walls or floors caused by settling or old age. There are great
cover-up materials for floors and walls that can be installed easily
and inexpensively. More serious defects should be handled by
someone who is an expert in structural problems.

Now is the time to replace corroded pipes or ductwork that is
in questionable condition. Before installing any new cabinets or
appliances, check the existing wiring and lighting. If your needs
have increased, or might within a few years, add the capacity now
to meet your new or anticipated requirements.

Wiring. Today's abundance of automatic food preparation con-
veniences calls for a generous supply of electricity in a kitchen.
To make certain that you will have adequate capacity in the wiring
system, check the wattage needs for the appliances you will be
using. Consider any possible increased requirements you might
have in the future. (For information on wiring, see page 120.)

Lighting and ventilation. While windows and doors contribute
natural light and can help to ventilate a kitchen, they can't provide the required amount of either. Kitchens need good general
illumination, preferably shadowless diffused light. In addition to
general illumination, there should be supplementary, glare-free
light for each work center, and subdued light for the eating area.

Unless the kitchen is properly ventilated, cooking odors will
permeate the entire house. If you have a special ventilation problem, or if you are building a new home, seek advice from someone
who is knowledgeable on the subject. (Various methods of lighting and ventilating a kitchen are discussed on pages 120 and 121.)

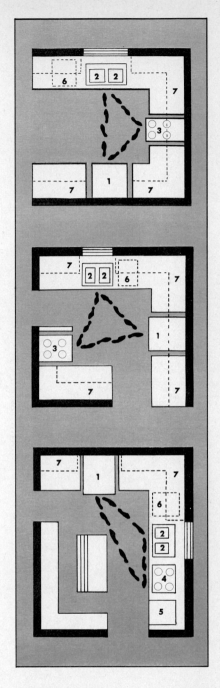

1. *Refrigerator*
2. *Sink*
3. *Freestanding range*
4. *Built-in cook top*
5. *Built-in wall oven*
6. *Dishwasher*
7. *Overhead wall cabinets*

The owners worked around existing features when they remodeled the kitchen in this 50-year-old home. Partitions that divided the room were removed, and cedar beams were installed across the 18-foot width. Original floor-to-ceiling cabinets were salvaged, and new cabinets, styled to match, were added. The sheet vinyl flooring enhances the washable wall covering, the decorative accessories, the tiffany-style lighting fixture, and the refinished table and chairs.

KITCHEN REMODELING

The first step in remodeling your kitchen is to make a detailed list of the items you need, in the order of their importance. You may find it isn't necessary to embark on a complete remodeling project that involves structural changes, new plumbing, and wiring. In many cases, remodeling can be accomplished within the existing space. Often, just the addition of one or more new appliances, better organization of storage facilities, a new floor, and more

Without making a single structural change, the 30-year-old, typically sterile-white kitchen below was updated to become the model of contemporary efficiency pictured at the left. The windows and all-tile walls were not changed, and new appliances and colorful cabinets were installed. A boxlike beam across the top of the windows improves their proportion, adds continuity to decorating, and houses lighting. Design on sheer curtain fabric matches wall covering on soffit. To conceal holes above sink where faucets once hung, tile stripped from another area was used. Hood above range vents through aperture where a wall fan was formerly placed. To avoid recessing, light fixtures are suspended from the ceiling.

adequate lighting, plus decorating will give you a kitchen that is not only more efficient, but more cheerful, too.

If you have to stay within a limited budget, in all probability you won't be able to fill all your needs immediately. Start by solving your biggest problems first, and so on down the list.

Once your kitchen remodeling project has been carefully planned, focus your attention on the most important aspects first, and don't let yourself get sidetracked. Many of the lesser projects can be done one step at a time as you can afford to do them.

Even if you don't have a handyman in the family, there are many areas of remodeling that can be done without professional help. It usually takes skilled craftsmen to build cabinets or to do plumbing or wiring, but almost anyone can do his own decorating or lay vinyl or carpet floor tiles. In order to find out just what your savings will amount to, ask your dealer to list separately the estimates for labor and materials.

If you hire professional help, find reliable people to do the job. While shopping, ask to visit kitchens that the company has done in other homes. Be sure to get an accurate floor plan and a complete list of materials and services in the price quotation.

TYPES OF KITCHENS

Before deciding what type of kitchen to have, you must find out exactly how much floor space you have. Then, analyze how your family lives, how you like to entertain, your kitchen work habits, and your hobbies. All of these elements will help you to determine what type of kitchen is best for you.

KITCHEN FOR FOOD PREPARATION AND SERVING

Some people prefer a kitchen that is used for food preparation and serving only. More often, this is apt to be the choice of a family of adults who prefer eating in the relaxed atmosphere of a separate dining room rather than in or near the kitchen work area. Others may have no other choice because of space limitations. In either case, this type of kitchen can be both functional and decorative. Usually, the most efficient arrangements for this type are a single-wall, galley, or U-shape. Plan the appliance placement carefully, and allow sufficient counter work space.

The kitchen below has facilities for food preparation and serving only. Even though it is small, this kitchen has clearly defined work center areas, located conveniently, and an abundance of storage space.

The pale blue of the cabinets, a wonderfully livable color, visually enlarges the small area. In the work center, the pink countertop and backsplash relate well to the blue cabinets. Resilient flooring, in an off-white, helps to maintain a light and cheerful atmosphere, and the wall of common brick, painted white, adds a great deal of textural interest.

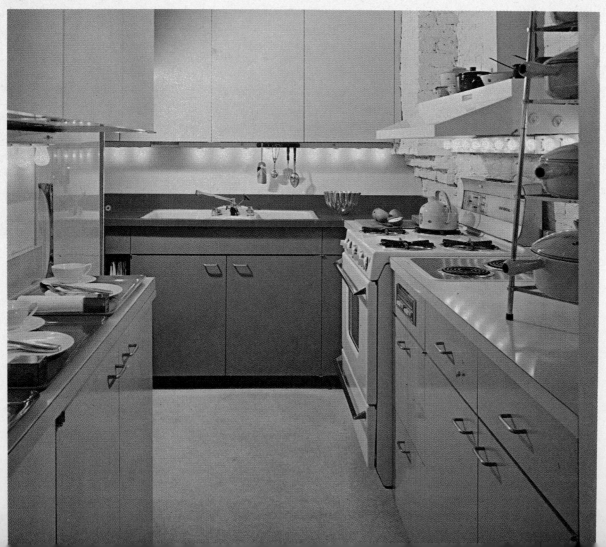

KITCHEN WITH BREAKFAST AREA

Most families enjoy having an eating area in the kitchen, even if it is only a snack counter or a small-scaled dinette table and chairs. Even those who appreciate dining in a more formal atmosphere in the evening are apt to gravitate toward the kitchen breakfast area early in the morning. This same spot may be equally popular for midafternoon or late-evening snacks. This is especially true if the kitchen has a warm, comfortable feeling.

For those who have small children, a kitchen breakfast area is almost a must. Food can be served quickly to hungry youngsters, and spillage and crumbs can be wiped up easily.

The breakfast counter in the kitchen above is located on two sides of the angled island. Breakfast cereals and informal pottery dinnerware are stored in the wall cabinet above the snack area so that morning meals can be served in a hurry. Recessed lights focus on the counter, which is covered with a yellow plastic laminate.

*This compact kitchen area (right) con-
solidates kitchen equipment so that
food preparation jobs can be handled
quickly and efficiently. Also notice
that illumination for each work center
is provided by a suspended fixture.*

*The lion's share of the total kitchen
space below is devoted to the eating
area designed for sociable, mealtime
get-togethers. The red and white
checked fabric at the windows and on
the table, red tiled floor, beamed ceiling, pots of greenery, and hanging
copper pots and pans all contribute
to the friendly, homelike atmosphere.*

COMBINATION KITCHEN-DINING AREA

Don't skimp on space when you plan your family's dining center.
From an efficiency standpoint, it's better to consolidate your food
preparation and clean-up centers into as small an area as is practical for the size of your family and the amount of equipment that
you must store, and to use the remaining space as a dining area.
Allow at least 24 inches of table or counter elbowroom per
person for comfortable dining. And leave plenty of leeway for
moving chairs, and for serving. Maintain at least 30 inches of
clearance around the table.

Some kitchens are too small to spare the space for an adequate
eating area, and can't accommodate a large enough counter to
serve the family. If this is your problem, the best solution is to use
adjoining space for informal meals or snacks. Sometimes, space
can be taken from an adjacent room, or can be adapted from part
of a remodeled garage or porch. If the dining area doesn't have an
easy and natural access to the kitchen, it's a good idea to include
a handy pass-through to facilitate meal serving. The pass-through
can be equipped with shutters or sliding panels to shut off the
view of the cooking center while meals are being served.

Another very practical way to plan your dining center is to install a buffet-peninsula as a divider between the kitchen and the
eating area. Have the storage space in the buffet open on the table
side so that dinnerware is easily accessible. Install adjustable
shelves so you can accommodate odd-sized and bulky items.

COMBINATION KITCHEN-FAMILY ROOM

If you and your family like to gather before meals to discuss the activities of the day while you and/or another person is preparing the meal, a combination kitchen-family room is the perfect choice for you. If you like to have comfortable furniture close to the kitchen so you can relax, this is the ideal place.

Comfort and convenience are of prime importance in a kitchen-family room. In order to have these features, there must be adequate space. If you're remodeling, remove the partition between the kitchen and an adjoining room to free space. If this is not feasible, incorporate the floor area of an unused back porch, a butler's pantry, or even a part of the back lawn.

Let the family room accommodate the features that are most important to your family. Be sure to include plenty of bookshelves if yours is a family that loves to read, and remember, too, that reading lights should be included in your plan. And, when possible, include a fireplace. This is more than just a luxury, as a softly glowing fire fills a room with friendliness and invites pleasant conversation. Also, let the dining table perform double duty—between meals, it can serve as a game table.

When you are decorating a kitchen-family room, use colors that are bright and friendly, and furniture that is casual and inviting. Add your own personal touch with accessories that include hobbies and/or collections, handcrafted items, and greenery.

The kitchen above is part of a combination kitchen-family room. The gentle angle in the kitchen wall cuts down a few steps during meal preparation. The eating counter has room for a pair of slide-under stools. A serving cart rolls where needed.

The glazed red tile used for the kitchen-family room floor and on the fireplace wall unifies the work center with the living area (left). The exposed wall supports and ceiling beams are given added impact by the addition of dramatically patterned vinyl-coated wall covering in bold colors. Shelves, built in between wall supports, hold books and decorative accessories.

COMBINATION KITCHEN-ACTIVITY ROOM

With the increased interest that today's families display for hobbies, crafts, collections, and games, a combination kitchen-activity room can be the most popular room in the home.

Because this room will, in all probability, receive more than a normal amount of wear and tear, be sure to keep uppermost in your mind easy-to-care-for features when you select the furnishings. Choose drapery and upholstery fabrics with a soil-resistant finish, tables and desk with a marproof surface, and floor covering that holds up well, regardless of the amount of traffic. Walls that are paneled, or covered with vinyl-coated wall covering, are also easy to maintain. Include a desk for home study and, if possible, a stationary game table and chairs. Be sure to provide ample storage space, either built-in or freestanding, to hold all the equipment that is necessary for family activities.

While a stereo system, TV, and telephone are welcome additions, the most important thing is a warm, friendly atmosphere.

The multipurpose combination kitchen-activity room below was designed to integrate family activities with the kitchen facilities. A built-in desk with wall-hung cabinets above makes a good home office because it is ideally located out of the line of traffic. There is plenty of room for hobbies, games, dining, and relaxing by the huge stone fireplace.

Stained oak beams bring decorative warmth to a textured, acoustical ceiling. Rough-sawn cedar paneling covers part of the fireplace wall, and rag rug carpeting covers the floor.

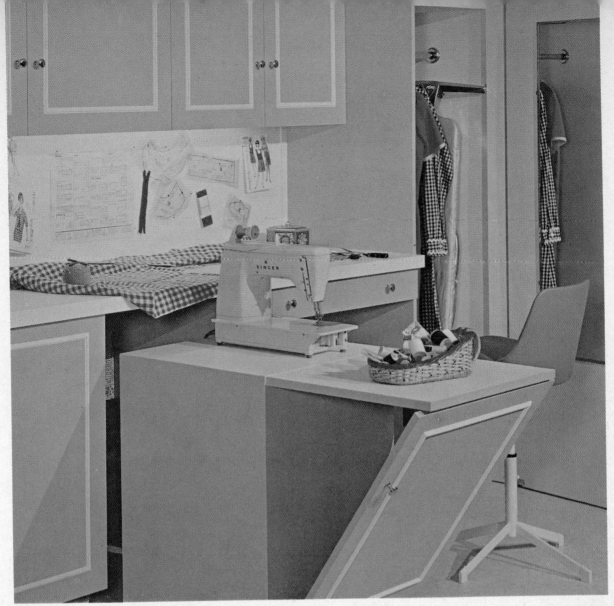

COMBINATION KITCHEN-SEWING ROOM

A corner or one wall of a large kitchen or adjacent family room, or a utility room nearby, makes a convenient location for a sewing center close to other family activities. Some sewing centers are merely space-saving units, either freestanding or built-in. Others are of a larger scale with more abundant work and storage space. If there's space for laundry appliances as well, let this area serve as a complete clothes care center.

If the sewing projects in your home are more than just the mending variety, you'll probably often have work in progress that you must put aside when you have other things to do. If this is so, include a sewing center in or near the kitchen. For women who like to sew, there's nothing more frustrating than having to dismantle and reassemble a sewing machine, material, and sewing supplies.

A big kitchen might include a sewing area, also, with this under-the-counter sewing center along one wall. It's just a large plywood box with a fold-up shelf on one side. The whole unit rolls out on casters, and it has a false door front to support the work shelf in the "up" position.

Cabinets above store materials for future projects. The pattern instructions and notions needed hang within easy view and reach, and fixtures recessed in the cabinets supplement the general background illumination, providing excellent working light.

To the right, a tall cabinet houses pressing equipment and has hanging space for garments being constructed.

Pictured below is a room that is truly wall-to-wall functional. Separate laundry wall adjacent to the kitchen concentrates two busy household activities in one convenient location. The attractive laundry is complete with storage cabinet for supplies, hampers to left of sink, and a tall cabinet with hanging space for clothes just removed from the dryer. Counter above appliances is ample for sorting and folding items. The small utility sink is used if any pretreatment is needed, and it also doubles for cutting and arranging flowers. Note the attractive and unusual window treatment, an automatic spirit brightener.

To the right of the tall cabinet is a desk area where cook books and laundry instructions are stored.

COMBINATION KITCHEN-LAUNDRY

Having a laundry near the kitchen is popular, and for good reason. It enables a homemaker to dovetail two of her busiest routine tasks—food preparation and laundry. It is a timesaving and step-saving convenience. An additional advantage of a laundry center near the kitchen is that it usually permits the sharing of the washer plumbing with that of the kitchen sink plumbing. This cuts the installation costs of appliances to a minimum.

If you are considering installing a laundry center in or near the kitchen, separate it in some way from the food preparation area. Plan the laundry niche for a corner, or separate it from the kitchen work area with a peninsula or an island.

A utility room adjacent to the kitchen also provides an ideal spot for laundry chores. If the utility room has an entrance from the yard or garage, it can function as a mud room, too. This encourages children to clean up after play. They also can change dirty or muddy playclothes and drop them into the hamper.

Wherever your laundry is located, plan it to be a bright and cheerful one. Bright colors in wall coverings, fabrics for window treatments, and floor coverings are great spirit lifters, and will help to keep laundry chores from becoming drudgery.

COMBINATION KITCHEN-HOME OFFICE

A desk or message center doesn't have to be large or elaborate. But it's handiest if located near the kitchen, close to where you spend a good portion of each day. This will put an end to searching for a recipe you clipped, a letter, or an instruction booklet. Plan a spot where you can file things in an organized fashion so you can find what you want, when you need it.

It can be as simple as an extension of a work counter, with drawer storage adjacent for items that go hand in hand with running a household. Cook books can be stored conveniently on the counter surface. Include a telephone to save you steps back and forth, and a bulletin board to keep messages posted in close view.

The corner desk niche in the kitchen above provides a relaxing spot for phoning, writing letters, or browsing through a cook book. On occasion, it becomes a study area for one of the children. Drawers store bills, clippings, correspondence supplies, and letters to be answered. Overhead cabinet houses paints, brushes, and earthenware items.

Concealed in the wall cabinet is a fixture that supplements the general background illumination, allowing shadow-free light for the desk surface. A yardstick of space is all it took for this handy kitchen-office.

chapter 2

KITCHEN STYLES

Convenience, comfort, and efficiency may be uppermost in your mind when you plan your kitchen, but there is another factor that also is important—style.

The kitchen style you choose—Early American, traditional, Mediterranean, Old English, contemporary, country, eclectic (a blend of many styles), or indoor-outdoor that can be adapted to any of the above styles—depends on certain basic factors: the architectural style of your home, the size of your family and the ages of your children, and the amount of time you spend there.

No less important are your individual habits and likes. Do you have family heirlooms that you want to display? If so, settle on a style that will enhance their beauty. Do you have interests or hobbies, or a job, that require a lot of time spent away from the kitchen? Then pick a style that requires a minimum of maintenance and upkeep. Is your kitchen clearly visible from other rooms? If so, it is wise to follow the same general theme as that in adjoining rooms. Or is it more or less isolated? If this is the case, you can choose a style that is a complete departure from that in the rest of the house.

An eclectic spirit is established in this kitchen by combining different styles. The contemporary cabinets are in direct contrast to the natural brick wall. Dishes, housewares, and accessories also are of many different materials and many different styles.

24

EARLY AMERICAN KITCHENS

When the owners of this home decided to add a family-dining room, they combined it with their small, outdated kitchen and carried out an Early American theme throughout the entire area. Salvaged brick, wood paneling, and the mellow wood tones of the cabinets are authentic reproductions of Early American design. These basic elements are further enhanced by the antique furniture and the interesting assortment of decorative accessories. The brick wall separating the family room from the kitchen works to advantage for both. Food can be put on the hooded grill from the kitchen side and served from the other side.

For many years kitchens patterned after those in early-day American homes have been one of the most popular choices with homemakers throughout the country. The use of natural materials projects an aura of warmth and hospitality and is reminiscent of the days of our forefathers when the kitchen was the hub of family activity. Now, when it is possible to add to this the convenience of modern appliances, heating, lighting, ventilation, and functional, built-in cabinets, the combination of the past and the present is the ideal solution for many homes.

A kitchen that consists primarily of wood, brick, and stone often is dark and cheerless. The same kitchen, however, if it is planned and executed in good Early American, is a perfect foil for brass, copper, pewter, and earthenware accessories, and colorful window treatments. A fireplace, even though it is not essential in the homes of today, is a highly desirable feature in an Early American kitchen because it creates a cozy atmosphere.

TRADITIONAL KITCHENS

Traditional styles, because they were influenced by the tastes of the reigning monarchs and by the work of prominent cabinet-makers, tend to be the more formal and sophisticated designs in home furnishings. This is true for kitchens, too, because kitchen styles are adapted from the more popular furniture styles.

If you have traditional English or French furnishings in your home, why not use the same style in your kitchen? Cabinets with paneled doors, traditional dining furniture, and crystal and china with a degree of formality can help to create this mood.

Queen Anne furniture beneath a hanging Tiffany-type lighting fixture, sparkling crystal stemware, formal china, and silver flatware establish a traditional feeling in the kitchen and dining area above. Stained birch cabinets are highlighted with bright yellow counters, and major appliances are grouped compactly. Above cabinets, artful objects focus attention on the ceiling.

MEDITERRANEAN KITCHENS

Mediterranean is a style that bridges the gap between casual colonial and elegant traditional styles. Its heritage is a mixture of many influences—most notably Spanish, Italian, and Greek. Woods used for Mediterranean furniture are usually dark, and surfaces are either paneled or carved. The look is massive and heavy. Tile floors with a Spanish motif, rough plastered walls, arched openings, beamed ceilings, and wrought iron furniture and decorative accessories set the stage for a Mediterranean kitchen.

Because it is a style that can be used in almost any room of the home, and because it can withstand more than the normal amount of wear, it is only natural that Mediterranean has become a popular choice for decorating and furnishing kitchens.

In the Mediterranean kitchen below, the cabinets have a natural wood finish in a dark tone, arched panels, and ornate hardware. The high ceiling with its massive beams, the chalk-white brick walls, and the vinyl tile floor with a Spanish motif add to the theme. White countertops, well planned lighting, and conveniently placed appliances add function to the room's decor.

CONTEMPORARY KITCHENS

Contemporary kitchens do not reflect one period, but rather a continual process of development. Designers of contemporary kitchen styles have been influenced by furniture designers of the past. There is a blending of function and aesthetics with the best use of today's materials—plastic, wood, glass, and metal. Designs are void of ornamentation and usually feature straight lines or floating sculptured curves. In a contemporary kitchen, cabinets may have a natural wood finish or a shiny enamel finish.

In the contemporary kitchen above, the bold colors in the washable vinyl wall covering set the pace for the decorating theme in the entire room. Each of the colors is picked up elsewhere in the kitchen, and the final result is a lively, but well-coordinated color scheme. Even the small appliances on the countertop, the canister set, and the other kitchen necessities add color as well as function.

COUNTRY KITCHENS

In this Country English kitchen, handsome oak cabinets with cathedral-raised panel doors provide authentic country feeling and charm. The hand-rubbed natural finish permits the graining to show to advantage, and the carving, deep moldings, and half spindles add a note of elegance. Brick walls and beamed ceiling are other features that add authenticity to the Old English atmosphere.

Country styles are direct descendants of traditional styles (although less ornate and sophisticated than the original styles), and are named after the geographical location from which they came. The most popular of these are Country English, Country French, and Early American. Even though they may vary somewhat in style and design, country kitchens always have a warmth that is particularly appealing. The basic time-honored natural building materials that have a part in everyone's past are partially responsible for the homeyness that country kitchens impart—wood cabinets with paneled doors, colorful tiles, ceramic countertops, plank or brick flooring, ceiling beams, and if possible a fireplace.

INDOOR-OUTDOOR KITCHENS

Indoor-outdoor kitchens actually are a type of kitchen rather than a style, but they are included in this section because they adapt so well to all of the kitchen styles. They are the ideal solution for families who enjoy "eating out" as frequently as the weather permits. Whether the food is prepared indoors or outdoors, it is quick and easy to move it to the eating area. And the garden view can be enjoyed from either indoors or outdoors.

One of the most popular ways to link a kitchen with the outdoors is to install a long set of windows in the kitchen and sliding glass doors between the two areas. However, with a great expanse of glass, you will probably want to install blinds, window shades, or draw draperies to reduce the glare when the sunlight is streaming in the windows. To lighten the chores of serving meals outdoors, it's also a good idea to install an outdoor shelf that you can use as a buffet ledge when you are entertaining.

This indoor-outdoor kitchen has close ties with two eating areas—one an attractive dining area indoors, and another a more carefree and casual eating-relaxing area directly beyond the sliding glass doors. Appliances have the appearance of built-ins, and are installed in an open plan that creates a feeling of spaciousness. The butcher's block in the center of the kitchen services all of the work centers, and is also an attractive addition. Bright yellow floor covering, draperies, and decorative accent pieces bring out the beauty of the cabinets' natural wood finish.

chapter 3

KITCHEN DECORATING

Decorating your kitchen involves more than hanging a new pair of curtains or adding a fresh coat of paint. Even a kitchen ideally planned for efficiency and function won't have a happy atmosphere unless a great deal of thought is given to its decorating. Good decorating is important for two reasons: it allows you to add light and color to a room, and it affords you the opportunity to add your own personal touch. What's more, if the decorating scheme is appealing to you, it's a little easier to get along without some of the extras that you've had your eye on—a new dishwasher or a side-by-side refrigerator.

Sometimes, it takes only one good idea to spark a whole roomful of changes. It might be a fresh coat of paint on the walls or cabinets, a brightly patterned vinyl wall covering, a new carpeting or resilient flooring, or a new lighting fixture.

On the pages that follow are suggestions for choosing decorative wall coverings, window treatments, ceilings, countertops and backsplashes, decorating kitchen cabinets, and selecting decorative accessories.

Colorful, washable wallpaper on wall and ceiling of kitchen at left keyed the color of midnight blue-painted cabinets and is coordinated with the ceramic tile backsplashes. The scheme is further highlighted by the collection of blue and white plates mounted on the wall.

32

WALL TREATMENTS

Color is the most powerful tool you have in decorating kitchen walls. You can key the wall color to the cabinets, to the counter-top surfacing, to the flooring, to the fabric used in the window treatment, to the ceiling color, to an outdoor view, or even to the colors that are visible in an adjacent room.

PAINTING KITCHEN WALLS

Painting is the least expensive way to decorate a kitchen wall. A fresh coat of paint gives a completely new look to a room that has grown drab and monotonous. Paint is available in a wide range of ready-mixed colors, or you can have a color custom-mixed at the paint store. If your kitchen walls have stubborn blemishes or you want to camouflage cracks, scratches, and spots, a spattered or stippled finish is your best bet. Even a novice can accomplish professional results by following simple instructions.

Choose the right type of paint. Basically, there are two different types of paint that are used on walls: One is alkyd (oil-base)

The home office area at the end of a small kitchen is painted in sun colors of yellow, lime green, and white. This mood is further enhanced by the orange canvas back and seat on the conveniently placed director's chair.

The kitchen area shown at the right is a good example of what paint can do to revitalize walls and old cabinets. The old hardware was replaced with white ceramic knobs, and the ceiling was covered with green-, yellow-, and white-striped wallpaper. Decorative accessories that include a collection of sunbursts and greenery, a white globe fixture, and stained shutters at the windows and door (not visible in the picture) complete the colorful redecorating plan.

and the other is latex (water-base). Oil-base enamel, in either a semigloss or high-gloss finish, is good for kitchen walls because it is impervious to practically anything, and it holds up well.

Water-base semigloss paint, called acrylic-latex enamel, is good because it has all the advantages of plain latex, yet it makes a hard-surface, washable finish. It is odorless, dries rapidly, and washes out of brushes and rollers with soapy water.

Select the right paintbrush. With few exceptions, follow this rule: natural bristles for oil-base paints, and nylon bristles for latex-base paints. You shouldn't use natural bristles for latex-base paints because the natural bristles will soak up the water and get very limp. Select a roller for the broad expanses of walls, and finish with a small brush in the corners.

Obtain other equipment that you will need. Besides the paint and the brushes and rollers, purchase a drop cloth, wiping cloths, sandpaper and/or liquid sander, masking tape, patching plaster and a putty knife to fill any cracks or holes, a paint scraper, and thinner and brush cleaner for oil-base paint.

Paint the woodwork first, then the ceiling, and then the walls. This suggestion applies if you are planning a complete paint job for your kitchen.

Preparation of the woodwork depends on the condition of the old surface. Remove all doorplates and hardware first. If the woodwork has a sound surface of semigloss paint, you can simply use liquid sander. This solvent removes wax and dirt and actually softens the surface of the old paint and helps the new paint adhere. Use the liquid sander as you paint, working ahead so you will paint the treated surface within a half hour or less. On woodwork that has previously been varnished, the liquid sander plus hand sanding is necessary. If the old woodwork is chipped, or has thick layers of paint, the only cure is to remove the old finish down to the bare wood before you apply the new painted finish.

If you are going to paint the ceiling, buy a roller that will accommodate a long handle so you don't have to stand on a ladder to reach the ceiling. You might want to consider one of the no-drip paints, which are made extra thick, in order to eliminate splattering. Use a small brush to paint in the corners.

Painting the walls is comparatively easy. Take down all pictures and wall hangings, and remove all picture hooks, nails, switch plates, and outlet cover plates. Do this even if you plan to paint the switch plates the same color as the walls. If you paint the walls without removing the plates, the next time you have to remove one to work on the electrical wiring, you'll peel off some of the paint at the same time.

Fill the cracks and holes with patching compound. Put it on with a putty knife, let it dry, and then sand smooth. Finally, scrub any especially dirty places with strong detergent solution, or turpentine for crayon or wax marks, and rinse with clear water. Then, paint the walls with a roller, using broad overlapping strokes. Cut into the corners with a small brush or roller.

Color runs rampant in the kitchen below. Cabinets and walls of bright orange enamel are teamed with red countertops, a patterned floor, and a white ceiling. Bold hues, like these oranges and reds, make a large room appear smaller. On the other hand, pastel tints are used effectively to make a small kitchen appear larger. Houseware items and major appliances, too, come in a range of bright or subdued colors that add to the fun of decorating your kitchen.

In the mini kitchen above, all the available area is put to work. A black and white cane pattern fabric is used effectively to cover the walls, cabinet doors, and the ceiling. When you use fabric to cover kitchen walls, be sure to protect it with a coat of acrylic spray so it will resist soil. The carpet in a light solid color helps to expand space, and the shallow cabinet and fold-down shelf put a dead wall to good use.

The theme-setting wallpaper in a striking pink-red color combination will retain its bloom because it's a vinyl-coated wall covering. If you look closely at the flowered wall, you'll see the refrigerator hiding behind matching panels of the same wallpaper. A chrome edging around each door secures a ¼-inch rigid panel that can be replaced whenever the decorating scheme is changed. The white backsplash, soffit, ceiling, and accessories add a sharp note of contrast to the dramatic pink and red combination.

WALL COVERINGS FOR KITCHENS

A wall covering will make a dramatic change in any room, especially in a kitchen where one or more walls may be devoted almost exclusively to cabinets. Along with its quality of setting the mood, a wall covering is practical as well. There are washable vinyl-coated wallpapers and vinyl wall coverings that range all the way from a dull matte finish to a shiny wet-look appearance. Many wall coverings are prepasted and pretrimmed. These are simple for the do-it-yourselfer to hang. Some are strippable, too. This makes them easy to remove from the walls.

Wall covering patterns are available in such a variety of designs and colors that it is no problem to find one that will add beauty to your kitchen. Prices vary according to design and quality (just as they do with almost everything you buy), but this doesn't mean you have to relinquish your dream of having the color and design of your choice, even if it is costly. If you have a limited budget, try covering one wall, or just use a wide wallpaper border on the soffit above the cabinets and extend it around the room.

Follow the same rules for choosing the color and design as you would in the rest of your home. Light colors will make a room appear larger, while dark colors will visually shrink it. Select a pattern that is scaled to the size of the kitchen, and avoid large designs if there are a lot of openings and cut-up areas to work

around. If the wall covering will be visible from other rooms, choose a pattern and colors that are compatible with the decorating scheme in the adjacent rooms.

Measuring for a wall covering is not difficult. Each roll contains 35 square feet. Narrow papers, between 18 and 20½ inches wide, usually come in double-bolt rolls. Wider papers, 28 inches, usually come in triple bolts. So, a wall ten feet wide and nine feet high requires three single rolls. When you shop for a wall covering, give your room's measurements to the salesperson so he can help you figure how much you'll need. Remember that you can deduct one single roll for every two ordinary door or window openings, but you must also add enough extra to allow for matching patterns.

Special characteristics that may determine your choice of wall covering—washability, colorfastness, plastic coating—are generally printed on the back of each roll by the manufacturer.

If you plan to hang a wall covering that is not prepasted, you will need a few simple tools. Wallpaper kits are very inexpensive, and they contain a paste brush, plumb line, hard roller, and a smoothing brush. The rest of the items—scissors, razor blade, paste bucket, and sponge—you probably have in the house.

If you have old wallpaper on the walls that must be removed before you hang the new wall covering, you no longer need to use the tedious method of scraping or steaming it off. There is a roller available that will do the removal job with a minimum of difficulty. It fits on a standard paint roller handle. Simply immerse the roller in warm, soapy water and roll it up and down the wall, soaking the wallpaper thoroughly. Metal ridges, spaced at intervals along the roller, perforate and drive water behind the paper to soften the paste. After waiting about five minutes, take a wall scraper and peel off the old paper.

Fill any cracks or holes with spackling compound or patching plaster and, as soon as they are dry, sand them smooth. For a more professional job, apply a coat of wall sizing.

Measure and cut the first strip of wall covering to size—the height of the wall plus four inches to allow for matching and trimming. As you cut the succeeding strips, match the pattern of each strip exactly at the right hand side of the preceding strip before you cut. Before you do any pasting, add a few drops of food coloring to the wallpaper paste so you can tell at a glance if the entire surface is covered. Brush the paste over half of the first strip, leaving an inch or two free of paste at the end. Fold the pasted end toward the center without forming a crease. Paste the other half and fold the same way. Trim the selvage.

Then, hang the wallpaper. Begin in a corner or at a doorway. First drop a plumb line to establish a perfectly vertical line for the first strip. When the paper is aligned, smooth it down, working from the top to the bottom. Match the pattern of each succeeding strip at the right hand side of the preceding strip. Use a seam roller to flatten down the edges. Then trim the excess paper at the ceiling and baseboard before the adhesive dries.

The washable wall covering in a deep blue and white tile pattern contrasts sharply with the dark-stained cabinets and woodwork in the kitchen above. Light-colored ceiling, countertops, and backsplash areas add light to the kitchen. The copper molds and a collection of brightly colored earthenware plates add both color and pattern to the decorating scheme.

Note also the double right-angled stainless steel sink that straddles the corner. This functional arrangement, which faces the window, allows the homemaker to enjoy the view of the patio that is just outside.

Important! *When you buy wall covering be sure to check the numbers on the back of each roll to see that they are all from the same dye lot. If they are not the same, there is a possibility that there might be a slight variation in color that will be noticeable after it is on the wall.*

The kitchen at the right illustrates the remarkable changes that can be made when you update an older home. This fifty-year-old home that underwent a complete remodeling job now boasts this exciting kitchen with its unusual combination of textures and materials. The walls, paneled in rough-sawn cedar with a hand-rubbed finish, provide an unusual background treatment for the mustard yellow wall cabinets and base cabinets in marigold that are of contemporary design. The rich color of the antiqued glaze tile on the backsplash complements the colors of the kitchen cabinets.

It's hard to believe that this kitchen is only 10x12 feet. Even though it is rather small, it appears larger than it really is because it has been thoughtfully planned to make the best use of every bit of space.

One feature that helps to create an expansive feeling is the acoustical tile and modular lighting panels in the nine-foot high ceiling. Another is the white laminated plastic countertops that add light to the kitchen.

An adjacent eating area with the same paneled wall treatment features a contemporary dining grouping along with choice antique pieces.

PANELING KITCHEN WALLS

There are many reasons why paneling is a wise choice for your kitchen wall covering. Besides providing an attractive background, paneling adds value to your home. It is durable, easy to maintain, and easy to install. It also is an excellent wall covering for problem kitchens, especially if you're faced with the task of repairing badly cracked or chipped plaster, or of removing many layers of old wallpaper. It is equally popular for new homes.

Today, the increasing popularity of low-cost 4x8 foot factory-finished wood paneling has provided an incentive for building supply dealers to offer an even wider selection of natural wood colors, complete with molding and trim to match. These panels are relatively easy to install, even for an inexperienced handyman.

Paneling is compatible with any kitchen style. It can be used for an entire kitchen, a single wall, or as a single panel that provides an accent to the rest of the room. Regardless of whether your home is old or new, or whether the walls are in good or poor condition, paneling offers the once-and-for-all solution. The baked-on finishes eliminate the need for further finishing and are guaranteed to retain their finish for a lifetime.

There are many types and styles of paneling to select from when paneling your kitchen. You can buy solid-wood paneling, plywood paneling with surface veneers of almost any species (unfinished or finished), and plastic-surfaced hardboard in various simulated wood grains or colors. There is even wallboard available that has overlay of paper or vinyl in many patterns and colors.

It is possible to install wall paneling with only a few ordinary hand tools, but the use of a power saw will speed up the operation considerably. (If you don't own one, you can always rent one by the day.) The only prerequisites for assuring a professional looking job are: 1. accurate measurements, 2. edges that are plumb or as close as possible together, and 3. common sense.

The first step is to prepare the walls. Be sure to check the wall for plumb, and to be certain that there is no loose plaster or other irregularity. If there is any extensive irregularity, repair it by patching it with plaster or spackling compound. Then, install furring strips on the wall to form a framework. This last step prior to attaching the paneling is more desirable than applying the paneling directly to an old wall.

The horizontal wood furring strips should be applied not more than 24 inches apart from floor to ceiling, and the vertical strips 16 inches apart or where the panel joints occur. If the wall appears "hollow" in some spots, level out with furring strips. Use cut steel nails or resin-coated nails to attach the furring strips to the plaster walls. If you are paneling a basement room, staple insulation batts between furring strips as a moisture barrier.

The next step is to lay out the job. Place the panels about the kitchen in order to plan the sequence for the desired grain and color effects. Arrange and rearrange the panels until you achieve the effect that pleases you most. For most interiors, it is wise to start in one corner and then continue working around the room.

The third step is the application of the panels. Much of the wood paneling is manufactured with tongue-and-groove joints, so there is no difficulty in joining them. Some others butt together and are prepared so that they form a simple V-joint. When this is not the case, make your own V-joint by running a plane along the edge of each panel before you start installing them on the wall.

If the paneling is to be attached with nails and the edges of the panels will be concealed with molding, batten, or posts, common nails can be used. If the nails will be exposed, use nails with heads that have been colored to match the surface of the paneling. However, all the nails should be applied ½ inch from the outside edges, spaced 6 inches apart at the top and bottom of the panels and 12 inches apart on the vertical edges of the panels.

On the other hand, if the paneling is to be applied with adhesive, be sure to read the manufacturer's recommendations that are printed on the label and follow them exactly. New adhesives make the job of fastening panels to the furring strips neater than nailing them. But do secure the panels with a nail in each corner. Then hold the panels with bracing until the adhesive is firmly set.

When all the panels are in place, add the matching ceiling and baseboard molding for the finishing touches to the job.

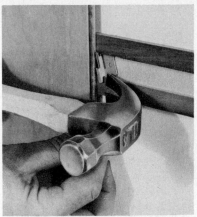

Top photo: *Use three- to five-penny nails to fasten furring strips to the studs. Use scrap pieces of furring to fill between strips at corners.*
Center photo: *Insert clips into the grooves, turning 90 degrees to lock them in place. Fit flange of clip over lip of plank. If it is snug, tap it with a claw hammer to drive the clips home. Nail through the clip to hold it firmly in place.*
Bottom photo: *Now, slip planks into place so that clips engage bottom lip of plank. Top lip conceals clips, forming V-joint with other plank.*

WINDOW TREATMENTS

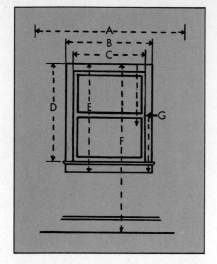

When measuring for curtains or draperies, measure from top of rod to sill, apron, or floor, depending on the length you want. Measure width from outer edges of fixture brackets or window frame. Add enough fabric to width for the return—distance of rod from the wall on each side.

To length, add hems. Lower hem should be at least 3 inches deep. Add 1¾ inches for upper hem, when a single hem is used. When a heading and casing are used, add at least 3¼ inches. The curtain should be at least two to three times as wide as the window, depending on sheerness of fabric.

Hand-printed fabric is featured in four-tier cafe curtains in the congenial eating area of the kitchen at the right. The same fabric is repeated in the shade of the hanging light fixture. Quaint accessories add to the homelike atmosphere of the room.

What to do about window treatments in the kitchen is not solved simply by hanging up some curtains. You may have a scenic view you want to enjoy, or you may have an ugly view you want to conceal. It may be you want to let in all the natural light, or that you want to regulate the light. Each situation has a solution.

If you want a window treatment that is truly something special, you can accomplish this quite easily. Even though you may feel that your windows are very ordinary, you can make them stand out if you discover how to utilize each window's good features.

The right window treatment will set the mood for the decorating scheme in the entire kitchen. There is a wealth of window treatment materials from which to choose; you can get spectacular results with surprising ease. In addition to kitchen window treatments that might first come to your mind—sheer curtains, cafe curtains, or draperies—there are many others you might like to consider. Take your pick of window shades—plain, trimmed, or laminated—that are either opaque or translucent, Roman shades, shutters, blinds, or even strands of beads.

MAKING CAFE CURTAINS

Cafe curtains are especially appropriate for kitchen windows and, for the homemaker who likes to sew, they are relatively simple to make. With the variety of fabrics available in both solid colors and patterns, it is possible for you to find just the right material.

Installing fixtures is the first step. Attach the cafe rod and bracket to the window frame, or mount a rod and socket inside the frame. And select from the variety of rings you can use on both types of rods—ornamental clips, pinch clips, or sew-on rings.

Taking measurements is the next step. Measure from the top of the rod to either the sill or the apron. If you are making cafe tier curtains, allow a 3-inch overlap. For hem allowances, and width of curtains, use the measurement chart on the preceding page.

One type of cafe curtain has a scalloped top. To make this version, you may use scalloped tape that is available in a 3-inch width. Place the tape on the right side of the fabric along the top edge. Stitch the tape ¼-inch from the scalloped edge. Cut out the scallops close to the edge of the tape and turn the tape to the underside and press the scalloped edge. Then stitch the lower edge of the scalloped tape to the curtain.

Or you can make a scalloped top without the pleater tape. Add 3 inches plus the seam allowance to the curtain length. Press back ¼ inch, then turn 1 inch at the sides of the curtain for the hems. Pin in place, and stitch. Press back ¼ inch on the lower edge. Then turn up a 3-inch hem, pin in place, and stitch.

Cut a facing strip 4 inches deep and the width of the curtain, plus the seam allowances. Use a nonwoven interfacing for the stiffening. Make a pattern for scallops on the interfacing. Divide the curtain width into fifths. There are usually six rings per curtain. Make a pattern of the scallop. Make scallops 1 inch apart, or shape to a point. Cut out scallop design to finished size on the interfacing, and sew to the facing. Sew the facing to the curtain top along the interfacing edge. Trim the seam to ¼ inch. Clip into the seam along the curve. Turn the facing to the inside. Turn under the seam allowances at the lower and side edges and press. Pin in place and stitch all around.

There are also fabric loops for hanging cafe curtains. Make the loops of self-fabric or contrasting tape and sew them into the seam as the facings are applied, or to the top of a straight hem. You can also make button-on fabric loops in round or pointed designs. Cut two pieces of fabric for each loop. Stitch the right sides together beginning at the narrow end of the loop. Make a ¼-inch seam. Leave one side open for about 1½ inches for ease in turning. Trim the seam to about ¹/₁₆ inch, turn the loop inside out, and press. Sew side opening together by hand. Stitch the narrow ends of the loops to the points of the scallops, and make a buttonhole in shaped end of each loop. Button loops over the rod.

You can also make a pinch-pleated heading for cafe curtains. Use pleater tape and drapery hooks at the top of the curtain. Then just hang the drapery hooks on the drapery rings.

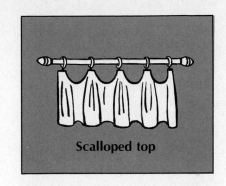

Scalloped top

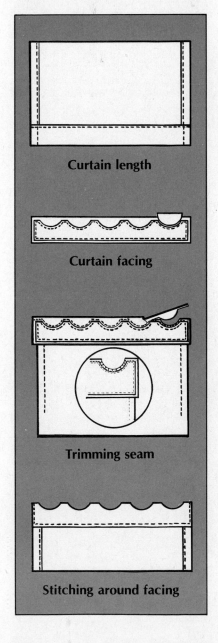

Curtain length

Curtain facing

Trimming seam

Stitching around facing

White shutters with movable louvers were chosen for the kitchen above. You decide how much light you want to let in. The same white is repeated in the laminated plastic countertops and backsplash areas, and contrasts with the green steel kitchen cabinets.

The white of the matchstick blinds and countertops acts as a cooling agent when it is combined with red steel kitchen cabinets and color-keyed wall covering. The hanging lighting fixture and the bowl of flowers repeat both the red and the white. Small amounts of black in the wall covering add a sharp note of contrast.

WINDOW SHADES

Use shades for a total kitchen window treatment, or in combination with cafe curtains, casement curtains, shutters, draperies, or valances. Whichever choice you make, you'll have an attractive window area, for there are colors and styles in either translucent or opaque shade materials to suit any decorating mood.

Keep texture in mind, too. If you have natural wood finishes in your kitchen, select a shade with a linenlike or burlap texture. Or if you have glossy enamel finishes, choose shades with a smooth surface. You can select from striped, patterned, or solid color materials. Each of these is available in trimmed or untrimmed versions, or with scalloped or shaped hems.

Trimming shades is not difficult, and can result in a truly custom look for your kitchen windows. You can buy inexpensive stock shades, have them cut to size, and add your own personal touch.

1. One of the simplest methods is to add rows of braid and fringe to shades. Choose colors that are keyed to the wall covering, cabinets, or decorative accessories. Attach the trim with glue that remains flexible when it dries, or use double-faced pressure-sensitive tape. Or, use press-on fringe or braid trim.

2. Appliquéd designs offer another way to add individuality to shades in your kitchen. Use the most important design in the pattern of a vinyl-coated wall covering or a tightly woven printed fabric. If you use fabric, spray the underside with an acrylic spray or outline the design with colorless nail polish before cutting it out. (This will prevent the edges from raveling.) Cut out each design carefully with small, sharp scissors. Place them on the shade in several different arrangements until you decide which one is most attractive. Next, apply glue to the underside of the design so that it is completely covered. Press each design firmly in place, and smooth each motif so there are no air bubbles between the shade and the appliqué designs. After the glue is dry, spray with an extra coating of acrylic spray over each design.

3. Laminated shades are a popular choice for those who desire a coordinated one-fabric effect. Use fabric that appears elsewhere in the room—cafe curtains, wall covering, cabinet door inserts, or seat cushions. Tightly woven fabrics such as cotton, linen, or rayon are best. If the fabric is thin or porous, the glue might show through. If the fabric is heavy, the shade will be too bulky when it is raised. This job is usually done by professionals, but there are several products that a homemaker can use to do her own laminating if she wants to economize.

4. Stenciled designs on window shades or valances offer another possibility for distinctive window treatments. The easiest way is to use a one-color stencil, as each additional color requires another stencil. Select a pattern or design used elsewhere in the room—floor or wall covering—and use it as a guide in creating your stencil design. Trace the design carefully and accurately. Then, transfer the traced design to heavy cardboard. Use a mat knife to cut out the design. Place the stencil on the shade and hold it in place securely with masking tape. Use textile paint, and apply it with a stencil brush held in an upright position. Use a circular motion as you work the paint into the stencil motif. If you are using more than one color of paint, be sure that the first coat of paint is thoroughly dry before applying the next color. After the stenciling has dried for 24 hours, iron it at low temperature to set the color. Place a pressing cloth over the design when you iron it.

SHUTTERS

Shutters are a natural for kitchen windows. They are available in a wide range of stock sizes, or can be custom-ordered in special sizes. They come in a variety of painted and natural wood finishes, or unfinished. Some panels are solid, or they may have movable or fixed louvers, or have stained glass, cane, mesh, or fabric inserts. Use any of these to cover the entire window area, or in combination with cafe curtains or valances.

BLINDS AND BEADS

These are other exciting materials you can use to brighten kitchen window areas. Blinds are available in wood, metal, aluminum, or bamboo with either wide or narrow slats that run horizontally or vertically. Regardless of the type of blinds you choose, they will be practical as well as decorative.

Strands of beads create sparkling kitchen window treatments that allow light to enter and air to circulate. The strands are available in many colors, shapes, and sizes in gem-cut crystals or opaque versions or natural wood tones, and are permanently fused to nylon cord. Cut them any length and mount on a bead track.

In the kitchen above, strands of glass beads that curtain the window are color-keyed to the striped wallpaper that frames the window and covers the ceiling. Pots of greenery on the window sill and a canister set on the counter repeat the same yellow, gold, and green color scheme.

The theme for the window treatment at the left is gingham and sunflowers. This is seen in the laminated window shades in the kitchen-dining area. The gingham shade is highlighted by bursts of tangerine sunflowers outlined in black, and topped with a valance made of the same checked gingham. The black braid trim and wrought iron shade pulls complete the window treatment. This theme also is picked up in the seat cushions and backrests of the wrought iron chairs, and is emphasized by the ingeniously executed sunflower-in-a-pot in the corner.

The stained glass windows in the kitchen below were salvaged from an old building, then installed above the sink during the remodeling of this 1890-vintage home. For a kitchen that has no interesting view, this is a novel solution to the window treatment problem, especially for an area that formerly was the butler's pantry. Also in keeping with the character of the house are the rich, dark-toned cabinets finished in plastic laminate paneling.

NOVEL WINDOW TREATMENTS

If you have a lovely view from your kitchen windows, but don't want any of the conventional window treatments, select a treatment that highlights the view. Surround the window with shelves to hold your cook books, or transform the window area into an indoor garden with greenery, or even an herb garden, in pots that flourish in the sunshine. Or, frame the window area with a collection of colorful plates mounted on the wall. For a very simple and effective low-cost window treatment, erect an awning over the window. Just make a scalloped canopy of sturdy fabric (denim, sailcloth, or other heavy cotton) and mount it above the

windows close to the wall; use a rod with a six-inch return at the bottom of the canopy (just above the scalloped edge) to hold it away from the window and maintain the awning shape.

If you have an ugly view, hide it. Create a stained glass effect with chunks of colored glass, broken into small pieces with a hammer, and glued to the window in a random effect with clear epoxy. Purchase the glass from a glass company and break it between two layers of paper or fabric to prevent flying splinters. Or buy a sheet of colored plastic cut to fit in the window frame over the glass panes. Mount a frame of plywood over the plastic.

Roman shades in the striking black and white kitchen above are made of the same fabric as that used for the panels in the cabinet doors and drawers. A matching valance that extends across both windows gives a finished look to the smart window treatment. Roman shades are regulated with a cord, rings, and pulley and fall into deep pleats when raised.

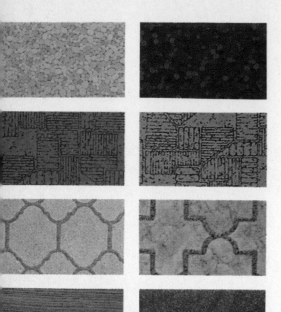

FLOOR COVERINGS

Because the kitchen is a heavy traffic area, it is wise to choose the best quality flooring you can afford. This is especially true of kitchens that have direct access to the outdoors. They are susceptible to grease, tar, sand, or gasoline. Fortunately, today there are more choices of types, styles, and colors than ever before, and many of the materials are easy to maintain. To select what is suitable for you—resilient flooring in either sheet or tile forms or carpeting—study the characteristics of these materials in the chart on page 46, and decide which is best for your home.

RESILIENT FLOOR COVERINGS

Resilient flooring comes in two basic forms—tile or sheet. You can buy individual tiles which you cement in place, or tiles with self-adhesive backing. In either case, they lend themselves to do-it-yourself installation. Sheet materials can be cemented for

The small samples above represent just a few of the many patterns that are available in smooth-surface flooring. An amazing range of colors and designs offers endless decorating possibilities for kitchens. Sheet flooring comes in 6-, 9-, and 12-foot widths. Floor tiles are 9 or 12 inches square.

In the kitchen at the right, vinyl flooring in a brick pattern was chosen for the kitchen area. This provides the same type of natural flavor as the slate floor used in the adjoining rooms. Fruitwood cabinets with authentic Provincial styling form a convenient "U" filled with storage space, and work-top room. Outside the "U," the far wall of the kitchen has a cooking center and a pantry to hold a large supply of canned goods.

The solid red carpeting in the kitchen and adjoining breakfast room at the left adds a note of sharp contrast to the glossy white cabinets. But, while the two areas are distinct, they are tied together effectively by the red dots in the lively contemporary vinyl-coated wall covering that sweeps across the ceiling, and by the red handles and hinges on the kitchen cabinets.

permanent installation, or can be installed loosely like rugs. It is the lack of seams that makes sheet flooring a real plus. There are no places for dirt to collect, so they are easy to maintain.

In selecting a hard-surface flooring, take into consideration not only the right color and pattern, but the durability, cost, ease of maintenance, and the type of installation. You will find that there are high-style patterns in all price ranges.

KITCHEN CARPETING

Kitchen carpeting is comfortable underfoot, colorful, durable, and easy to maintain. It comes in solid colors, plaids, stripes, geometric designs, and floral patterns. Of the many types available, multicolored patterns or tweeds show soil less than solid colors; the trim tufted or flocked carpets with tightly constructed, short, dense loops are easiest to maintain. However, the dark shades, with the exception of the very deep shades of carpet that show lint and surface dust more readily, tend to stay fresh-looking longer. Especially good soil concealers are the medium golds, browns, greens, and blues. They would be the most practical choice in homes with pets and/or small children. Kitchen carpeting comes in 6-, 9-, and 12-foot widths and also in carpet tiles.

The carpet samples pictured below are only a few examples of an exciting big group of carpets geared to use in kitchens and family rooms, and other areas where special wear properties are desirable. You will find colors, textures, and patterns to suit any style or any decorating mood.

OTHER KITCHEN FLOOR COVERINGS

Glazed tile, brick, marble, travertine, flagstone, pebbles, wood, and other natural materials are sometimes the choice for kitchen floors. Wood, covered with a heavy coating of clear vinyl is practical as well as beautiful for a kitchen floor. It comes in a variety of precut shapes. There is also a liquid flooring that you just pour over any old material—cement, linoleum, wood—that is impervious to stains, moisture, or abrasion.

FLOOR COVERINGS—TYPES AND CHARACTERISTICS

Types	Resilience	Resistance To Grease, Alkali, Staining	Durability	Key Advantages	Ease of Maintenance
Asphalt tile	Poor	Poor	Very good	Low cost	Fair
Brick	Poor	Poor	Excellent	Natural beauty, durability	Fair
Carpet	Superior	Good	Very good	Quiet and comfortable underfoot	Good
Ceramic	Poor	Good	Excellent	Durability	Good
Cork tile	Excellent	Fair	Very good	Quiet underfoot	Good
Cork tile—vinyl	Good	Good	Excellent	Quiet underfoot	Excellent
Linoleum	Good	**(Grease)** Superior **(Alkali)** Fair	Very good	Low cost, easy to maintain	Excellent
Rubber tile	Excellent	Good	Very good	Comfort underfoot	Good
Seamless poured floor	Good	Excellent	Very good	Endless design possibilities	Very good
Vinyl— asbestos tile	Fair	Excellent	Excellent	Low cost, easy to install	Excellent
Vinyl— cushioned sheet	Superior	Excellent	Very good	Quiet and comfortable underfoot	Excellent
Vinyl-rotovinyl	Excellent	Excellent	Very good	Low cost, requires no adhesive	Excellent
Vinyl—sheet	Good	Excellent	Excellent	Wide selection of patterns	Excellent
Vinyl tile-solid	Fair	Excellent	Very good	Durability, easy to install	Good
Wood	Good	Fair	Very good	Durability, beauty	Good

CEILINGS

Once, kitchen ceilings were strictly functional, and usually were painted white or a pastel tint. Now, they can have decorative appeal with the aid of many new materials, and they can be effectively integrated in the decorative style you desire by the use of paint or wallpaper, or by installing beams or acoustical panels. But before you attempt to decorate your kitchen ceiling, check it carefully and have any damage corrected. Ceiling cracks are the most common fault. They are usually the result of normal settling. They can be repaired easily with patching plaster, and then decorated with whatever material you desire.

A brilliant floral wallpaper in raspberry, royal blue, and leaf green creates a ceiling bower in the kitchen above. A companion border adds scalloped trim to the soffit. The same shade of raspberry is repeated in the cabinet countertops, and all of the ceiling colors reappear in the Tiffany lighting fixture. Another pattern appears on the kitchen floor—vinyl brick flooring in a distinctive design. Even the spices in the wall-mounted spice racks restate the colors that are used in the ceiling.

PAPERED CEILINGS

The time-honored method of papering ceilings is still popular today. But now the materials at hand are washable and easy to hang. Most popular is vinyl-coated wall covering. Some are pre-pasted and strippable. However, today you can cover the ceiling with the same material you use on the walls, or you can have a papered ceiling that complements painted or paneled walls. Make your selection from a vast collection of colorful designs.

PAINTED CEILINGS

Painting is the quickest and least expensive way to refinish ceilings unless you have some special problems. Use the same preparation technique as you would for walls. (See page 32.)

BEAMED CEILINGS

A wood-beamed ceiling in a kitchen is a way to gain overhead drama. Use synthetic beams that closely resemble hand-hewn beams, or select from boxlike vinyl beams that fasten to wood strips nailed to the ceiling, or lightweight plastic foam beams.

Wallpaper with poppy red, orange, and lavender flowers covers the ceiling in the kitchen above and creates a charmingly flower-strewn effect overhead. The scalloped wallpaper border visually lowers the high ceiling, and a wallpaper valance, the same size and scallop as the border, continues the line across the top of the window. Floral motifs, cut from fabric matching the wallpaper, were applied to the citrus green window shade in a random design.

The rustic ceiling beams in the kitchen at right are in keeping with the authentic Colonial decor of the rest of the house. The brick floor, chestnut cabinets, and antique decorative accessories all add to the character of this remodeled kitchen.

ACOUSTICAL CEILINGS

Acoustical ceilings have many advantages for use in the kitchen. Not only are they sound absorbers—when properly installed they absorb between 55 and 75 percent of the sound waves striking them—but they are easy to clean and maintain. These are definite pluses for kitchens with many noise-making appliances and much smoke that normally swirls and dirties the kitchen ceiling unless you have the most advanced range exhaust fan.

Essentially, acoustical ceilings are of three types: suspended, tile, and plank. Some have a vinyl coating that resists grease; all will retain their new look for years. All three types are relatively simple to install for anyone who is handy with tools. Or, you may elect to have the work done by professional installers. If so, ask your local building supply dealer to refer you to someone who is competent and charges a fair price.

Suspended ceilings have gained acceptance in kitchen remodeling for a number of reasons. They offer an inexpensive way to lower old-fashioned high ceilings; to cover unsightly wiring, ducts, and pipes; and to conceal cracked and peeling ceilings.

A lightweight metal framework suspended from the ceiling joists, with a wall molding at the new ceiling height, supports the modular-size panels. If you want no-glare lighting, you can install fluorescent lighting fixtures over luminous panels that can be incorporated into the ceiling grid system. If it is necessary to make repairs to the wiring, ducts, or pipes after the suspended

The kitchen above has a suspended ceiling of luminous panels with fluorescent lighting fixtures installed above the panels. The vinyl wall covering with splashy yellow flowers reaches across the ceiling to meet the floating panel of light.

The modular light squares are repeated at an angle in the vinyl floor covering. This uniform feeling of light and spaciousness and the sunny color scheme are continued in the clear yellow countertops, white cabinets with yellow molding, yellow- and white-checked gingham cafe curtains, and yellow and white furniture and accessories.

The drawing above illustrates how you can staple acoustical tile directly to gypsum board. Here's how to do it: Drive a staple through tile flange into ceiling. Without moving staple gun, drive a second staple directly over the first. The first staple causes the prongs of the second to flare out into the gypsum board, locking the tile securely in place.

In the kitchen below, good general lighting is achieved with a full luminous ceiling. Although the kitchen is small and windowless, this type of lighting imparts a feeling of natural daylight in the entire kitchen. The light-colored floor, countertop, and backsplash also add light. The cabinet doors and drawers are covered with a blue floral vinyl wall covering.

ceiling is installed, they are easily accessible. Simply remove the proper panel to get at the problem area, make the necessary repairs, and then replace the ceiling panel.

To install a suspended ceiling, first determine the height of the new ceiling and mark this point by snapping a level chalk line around the perimeter of the kitchen. Then, attach the molding to the wall, using the chalk line as a leveling guide.

The next step is to screw steel eyelets into the joists or existing ceiling at 4-foot intervals. Next, attach the hanger wires to the eyelets. Bend each of the wires at the point where they intersect the reference strings you've installed 1⅛ inches above the wall molding. These reference (or leveling) strings should run along one short wall and one long wall of the room.

Now you're ready to install the first main runner. Do this by resting one end of the runner on the wall molding and then fastening the other end of the runner to the bent wire. Twist the wire several times to secure the loose end. Once this is done, you can start working your way back along the runner, fastening the hanger wires every four feet. By doing this, you can provide added support for the runners. Continue with this procedure until all of your main runners are installed and secured.

The fourth step is to install 4-foot cross Ts between the main runners you have secured. Place these cross Ts at 24-inch intervals. This may vary if your panels are of a different size. Once the Ts are placed, you can insert the end tab into the main runner slot. Then all you have to do is to push it to lock. Your framework is complete, and you now have a sturdy grid system.

You can now lay the ceiling panels into the grid by tilting the panel edges slightly upward, then sliding slowly through the opening. Work slowly so you won't break or chip the edges of the ceiling tile. Once the panel is through the open grid, rest it on the grid flanges. Follow this procedure with the other tiles.

Tile or plank acoustical ceilings may be installed by one of three methods—cementing, stapling, or nailing. The installation method you select depends on two things: the condition of your ceiling and how much headroom is available.

If the present ceiling is in relatively good condition, the fastest, easiest, and most economical method is to cement the tiles or planks right to the existing ceiling.

But if the ceiling is badly cracked or uneven, the stapling method is best. Start by nailing 1x2-inch wood furring strips at right angles to the ceiling joists. Space them on 12-inch centers for 12x12-inch tiles, so that all the tile joints will occur over the strips, keeping them lined up properly. A special tongue-and-groove joint conceals the staples and ensures a level ceiling. It takes planning, but instructions included with tile will guide you.

Dry-wall panels work well on ceilings and are less expensive than ceiling tile. They are harder to install, however, since you have larger panels to handle. Cut the panels to size, nail them up, tape the joints, and then paint them to finish the job.

COUNTERTOPS AND BACKSPLASHES

Installing a countertop and a backsplash is a good way to create a new look in your kitchen. But be sure that the pattern and color that you select fits into your kitchen decorating scheme.

There are many materials to choose from. Linoleum is a good choice because of its durability. It is available in many colors and patterns. Use $\frac{1}{16}$-inch gauge. Formica and other high-pressure laminated plastics are also excellent choices. They resist stains, heat, abrasions, moisture, and fading. Use $\frac{1}{16}$-inch gauge. Another common material, vinyl, is available in various thicknesses, and resists alcohol, stains, moisture, abrasions, and heat up to 275° F. If you want a small-tile effect, use ceramic tile. Available mounted on paper sheets, it resists heat, water, stains, and small cuts. Laminated hardwood, too, is available for a patterned effect. It resists heat up to 382° F. For a clear look, use stainless steel. While this cannot be used as a cutting surface, it will resist abrasion and will not chip, rust, or tarnish.

INSTALLING A COUNTERTOP

Unless you want a countertop of laminated plastic, which is best left to a professional, this is a job that you can do yourself. Check with your local rental agency for any tools you may need. Then check with your building supply dealer on the number of tiles you need if you are installing ceramic or quarry tile. Make sure you have special tiles for the counterfront and corners.

Make sure the present countertop is structurally sound; or if you are installing a new one, make a frame of ¾-inch plywood. Then lay the tile. Small ceramic or quarry tiles are mounted on strong, flexible backings. These are the easiest to handle. Cut and fit the tile by starting at the front edge. Make the first row of bullnose tile overhang the base cabinet by ¼ inch. Line up the front edge flush with ¼x1-inch-deep wood chamfer strip. Press tiles firmly on surface spread evenly with waterproof ceramic tile floor-type adhesive. Let it dry, then fill the joints.

To insert marble, ceramic glass, or ceramic tile, check the thickness of the material to be inserted. Rout out the area with a ½-inch bit and an electric drill. Put the insert in place.

INSTALLING A BACKSPLASH

First, clean the surfaces to be covered and cove the area between the counter and backsplash. Secure all loose edges and fill cracks. Before installing backsplash, remove fixtures and switch plates.

If you are covering the backsplash with vinyl wall covering or wallpaper, use the adhesive suggested by the manufacturer.

If you are using ceramic tile in a plain or textured finish, buy those that have a protective peelable film.

When covering new walls, prime the plaster or plasterboard with an oil-base primer or a coat of varnish.

In the top photo, textured ceramic glass that resists heat, water, stains, and small cuts is set into a colorful laminated plastic countertop. The backsplash is covered with vinyl floor covering in a single-brick pattern that adds textural interest.

In the bottom photo, the countertop is covered with wood-grained laminated plastic; the backsplash is covered with textured ceramic tile.

DECORATING KITCHEN CABINETS

In the Old English kitchen below, handsome oak cabinets, with cathedral raised panel doors, provide authentic country feeling and charm. The desk unit, part of the same grouping, has a green stained finish, while the kitchen cabinets have an oak finish. The hand-rubbed natural finishes permit the graining to show to the best advantage.

When you're trying to decide how to finish your kitchen cabinets, first visit the kitchen cabinet showrooms in your area, and look at the kitchens in model homes and in those of your friends. But don't be swayed by the first glorious array of colors, wood finishes, or sculptured laminates you see. Explore every source, regardless of the amount of money you have budgeted for this project.

WOOD FINISHES

Because kitchen cabinets occupy a major portion of the space available in your kitchen, represent a large expenditure of money, and have a degree of permanency, the type of finish you choose is an important decision. The natural finishes can be light or dark, the woods heavily grained or sanded smooth. If an antique finish appeals to you, you can combine both color and texture.

Here are instructions for applying finishes on five kinds of wood cabinets: walnut, pine, oak, maple, and fir. Whether your cabinets are solid stock or plywood, the finishing process for each kind is the same—maple plywood takes the same finish as solid maple, and so on. Whatever finish you use, it's a good idea to practice on a small piece of scrap stock of the same material, or on an inconspicuous part of the cabinet. When you're satisfied with the results, use the same technique on the cabinet fronts.

1. Walnut. Walnut stays light beneath an all-lacquer finish. Rub between coats. Varnish and clear resin sealers darken walnut. Unless it is exceptionally open-grained, walnut will smooth out under successive coats of varnish or lacquer, without a filler. If you use a filler, you can tint it with raw umber.

For a stained walnut finish, use walnut stain. If you want to keep the stain a light color, wipe quickly, dilute the stain, or apply a thinned coat of synthetic resin sealer before you stain. Seal the stain with a coat of shellac or clear varnish.

2. Pine. This is the easiest finish of all—but the golden, light brown color doesn't come until the wood has been exposed to light for several months—or years. Brush on boiled linseed oil. Let it penetrate for an hour or so—then wipe it off, and wax.

For an antique pine finish, apply a wash coat of orange shellac (4-pound cut diluted with six parts of alcohol). Mix a weak wiping stain of raw sienna in linseed oil. Darken it slightly with raw umber, if you wish. Brush it on, and wipe it off after a few minutes. Finish with a coat of clear, low gloss varnish.

3. Oak. Oak often runs less true to color than most new woods and may need bleaching for natural oak finishes to equalize colors. After bleaching, sand, dust, and fill with neutral paste filler. To retain the natural look, finish with shellac, lacquer, or varnish. Interesting variations can be achieved by mixing a tint of brown, red, or green in with your wood filler.

4. Maple. Sand first, then dust. Use lacquer or white shellac or synthetic resin sealer. Then build up the lacquer or varnish finish, and apply a coat of wax. For a Colonial maple finish, apply a coat of stain, and wipe. Let it dry thoroughly. Then finish off with successive coats of clear varnish.

5. Fir. It is not necessary to sand fir. Brush on synthetic resin penetrating filler—one coat or two, depending on the degree of staining desired. Buy wiping stain of the desired color, or make your own by diluting enamel or oil-base paint with turpentine or oil. Brush on, then wipe off. Blend out, wiping selectively, for the desired result. Finish with two coats of varnish.

The cabinets, walls, and ceiling in the kitchen above are simply constructed of wood stained in a warm, natural finish. This treatment provides a perfect background for a large collection of antique accessories.

The cabinets in the kitchen below feature an unusual decorative treatment. Mahogany strips, spaced ½ inch apart, overlay black lacquered mahogany cabinets that feature contemporary styling.

Opening a cabinet door in the kitchen below is like reaching for a whole bouquet of garden-fresh flowers. The owner painted the designs on the cabinets, and finished them with a coat of clear lacquer for durability.

PAINTED FINISHES

You have access to an artist's palette when you decorate your kitchen cabinets with paint. Not only can you take your pick of a full rainbow of hues, but also of cabinet styles to team them with. You can key the color of the cabinets to the wall covering, window treatments, floor covering, countertop material, or decorative accessories. You'll enjoy mixing and matching colors to create a fresh, new color scheme for your kitchen.

When you paint the kitchen cabinets yourself, remove all of the hardware first. For cabinets with a sound surface of paint, you need only to use liquid sander. Follow up with fine sandpaper (120 grit) until all traces of the gloss are gone. If the cabinets are varnished, a good, complete hand-sanding following the use of a liquid sander is recommended. If the cabinets are new, apply an undercoat first. Brush on two coats of good-quality enamel, let it dry thoroughly, and replace the hardware.

In the apartment kitchen above, the old kitchen cabinets were finished with bright blue enamel, and the old knobs and drawer pulls replaced with new white china pulls and knobs. This attractive mood was continued in the antique medicine chest at the right of the cabinets.

56

The cabinets in the kitchen at the right were given a custom touch by decorating them with original designs done in papier-mâché and trimmed with rope and then treated to an antiqued finish in a natural wood-tone. And the door panel at the end of the kitchen was brightened by nailing flattened tin cans from Spanish olive oil, Danish sausage, English breakfast syrup, Japanese oatmeal, and Indian curry to gold leaf background.

The old outmoded cabinets in the photo below were completely renovated and updated. First, sculptured motifs were glued on the door and drawer fronts, and then the cabinets were antiqued with a wood grain kit. The old hardware was replaced with new brass pulls, and a bright orange laminated plastic countertop and backsplash were installed.

SCULPTURED MOTIFS AND MOLDINGS

There are sculptured plaques, medallions, and moldings that can be applied to kitchen cabinet doors and drawers to create a unique decorative effect. These distinctive carvings have the elegant look of hand-carved wood, but are machine-made and are much less expensive; they add an exciting new dimension to kitchen cabinets that have no particular design features. You can buy them in a variety of sizes and designs at your building supply dealer or paint and wallpaper store. There are round, oval, square, and rectangular shapes as well as strips of premitered moldings that come in several widths and lengths. These decorative motifs and moldings are made of synthetic materials that have permanent dent-resistant durability and resiliency.

First, prepare the cabinets for the finish you plan to use. (See pages 52-55.) Then, attach the motifs and moldings to any flat-surface doors and drawers with neoprene adhesive or, after pre-drilling, nail or screw them in place. Now, finish the cabinets with stain, paint, or an antique finish to match your kitchen decor. You can use these same motifs and moldings on kitchen doors and cornices over the windows.

DECORATIVE TRIM

There are so many ways to add decorative interest to ordinary kitchen cabinets without embarking on extensive remodeling.

If you have walls and/or ceiling papered with vinyl-coated wall covering, cut out motifs or borders and attach them to the cabinet doors with adhesive in a pleasing arrangement. For cabinets that need a fresh coat of paint, do this before you add the designs and key the paint color to one in the decorative trim.

If you have kitchen cabinets with paneled doors, cover the panels with wall covering fabric that matches the shades or draperies, or self-adhesive decorative covering. Use either a material with a bold or colorful design or, for a solid color, choose one with texture such as burlap, grass cloth, or a tweedlike material. If the panels are removable, have a different treatment on each side of the panels and reverse them whenever you feel you need a change in your kitchen decor. Or, for still greater variety, replace the panels with translucent plastic panels that resemble stained glass and come in a variety of colors and patterns. These can be cut easily with a hacksaw, and installed just as easily.

Sometimes, just replacing the old doorknobs and drawer pulls with new hardware will give outmoded cabinets an up-to-date look.

For cabinet doors that are outlined with a narrow molding, paint this in a contrasting color that appears elsewhere in the kitchen — window treatments, wall covering, or countertop. Or, cut panels of felt and glue inside the moldings with spray adhesive. Buy an assortment of tin molds and fasten them to each panel.

Here's a high-style, low-cost idea for decorating kitchen cabinets that is simple to do. Posy-pattern vinyl-coated wall covering is splashed on the ceiling with a few flowers trailing off onto the cabinet doors. These motifs were cut from the ceiling paper and glued to the doors. Then, a protective coat of clear lacquer was applied to add durability.

A highly imaginative use of gift wrap paper has been used in decorating the cabinets in the kitchen at the left. The rolls were cut out and pasted to the plain white cabinets. Then, a coat of clear plastic was applied to make the decoration long-lasting.

The outdated kitchen above, which always seemed to be in need of a coat of paint, was transformed into the contemporary one at the lower right. This was accomplished by a nonprofessional handyman in just one weekend. New suede-finish laminated Plastic door and drawer fronts—precut, predrilled, and factory-engineered for each installation—were used in the kitchen cabinet face-lifting that required only a few hand tools, an ordinary electric iron, and accurate measurements. This is an ideal shortcut that allows you to rejuvenate old cabinets for easy-care maintenance without the expense of buying new cabinets.

If you're looking for a fast, easy, and economical way to restyle your old kitchen cabinets, here's a shortcut that lets you restore outmoded cabinets without replacing or refinishing them. Simply apply a decorative trim to the cabinets.

The secret is suede-finish laminated plastic fronts—precut, predrilled, factory-engineered for each job, packaged, and shipped complete with hardware. And they cost only a fraction of the amount of installing most new cabinets. Even if you're not very handy, you should be able to remodel most wood or metal cabinets.

All you need are a few hand tools and an electric iron. Take an accurate overall measurement of your existing cabinets in the kitchen, and decide which of the wood-grain finishes you want.

There's no need to measure each door and drawer. Simply diagram the storage, then mark the dimensions on the diagram to the center line between the drawers and doors. The factory will take over from there, designing and manufacturing all new fronts so they are easy to install and fit perfectly. No hard-to-handle adhesives or high-speed cutting tools are necessary for installation.

Use an electric iron to bond the special matching laminate onto permanent surfaces—ends of cabinets, metal sink front, and framing strips. The laminate that is included in the package with the door and drawer fronts is heatproof and pressure sensitive.

To fit unusual shapes or contours, mark (scribe) the edge, then score with a linoleum knife. Peel off the paper backing, and bend slowly along the scored line. Add your favorite pulls and molding if you wish, or choose from several available options.

A lush green and white color scheme gives the kitchen above an inviting outdoor look. White lattice panels cut from vinyl-coated fabric are used to decorate the reversible cabinet door panels. The same colors are used in the cane pattern wall covering and the striped Roman shades.

Black wrought iron door and drawer pulls and H-hinges add just the right finishing touch to the warm, mellow tones of the knotty pine kitchen cabinets pictured above. Designs such as this are faithful reproductions of hand-wrought hardware. The maple furniture, vinyl flooring with brick design, and antique decorative accessories complete the convivial setting.

HARDWARE FOR KITCHEN CABINETS

Be sure to select the hardware for your cabinets early in your project plans. In addition to selecting a design you admire and one that is compatible with your cabinets, select also that hardware which functions best for you. Do you prefer a pull or a knob? Which will be most convenient for you to use? And where should you position it if cabinets are to be custom-made?

No matter what style of kitchen cabinets you plan to have, or what type and color of finish they will have, there are hardware designs that are appropriate. You will find both door and drawer pulls and knobs in several sizes in tradition, country and contemporary designs. There is also a variety of materials and finishes to make your selection from—antique brass or copper, wrought iron, wood, china, and silver. You can also get hinges to match whatever design cabinet hardware you choose.

If you're replacing your old knobs and pulls with hardware of a similar type and size, the same holes can be used again. If not, you will have to fill the holes with wood filler, sand, and refinish the doors. Metal doors can be decorated with molding or vinyl to conceal the old holes. Before you start out to buy new hardware, double-check the measurements for pull hardware. The size is measured from center to center of the hole openings.

Nos. 1, 2, and 3 *are distinctive shapes and designs of door pulls from Mexico. These have different combinations of semiprecious stones and brass that make each piece interesting in its own right. They can be purchased in import shops, and are especially appropriate with wormy chestnut cabinets.*

No. 4. *These drawer and door pulls are made from German springerle cookie molds that can be purchased in houseware departments.*

No. 5. *"Figure" door pulls, such as this one, will add a custom look to louvered wood-tone cabinet doors, and others of simple design.*

No. 6. *The stone slab door pulls on these kitchen cabinet doors are made from African tiger eyes. They are completely individual, no two alike.*

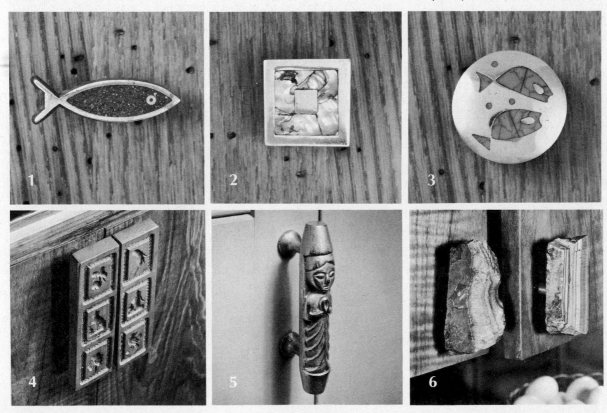

DECORATIVE ACCESSORIES

The dramatically simple, clean lines of the contemporary kitchen below offer an ideal background to show off a collection of hobbies and crafts. This is an excellent kitchen for the lover of antiques, ceramics, and weaving to display his collectibles. Your family's hobbies may be different, but you can create a special, very personal look by displaying them in an equally effective manner.

In many cases, the kitchen is the most lived-in room of the home. Beyond the everyday tasks such as meal planning and preparation, it can be a center for entertaining guests, a haven for experimental chefs, a home office or a hobby workshop, or even a play area for the children. Because families do spend so many enjoyable hours there, it is most important for the kitchen to be equally as attractive as it is efficient. With the addition of family possessions, displayed effectively, you can create a pleasing atmosphere in your kitchen that is completely individual.

Along with items that are purely decorative, you can also bring out into the open your cook books, cooking utensils, and dinner-

ware so that they are readily accessible. You can combine both decorative accessories and useful items on open shelves and establish a warm and inviting look in your kitchen. When you plan your decorative accents, make use of wall hangings; kitchen tools, pots and pans; a clock; family heirlooms and collections; fruits; vegetables and greenery; and creative kitchen crafts.

WALL HANGINGS

The amount of wall space you have in your kitchen, whether it is painted, paneled, tiled, or covered with a patterned wall covering, will determine the number and type of wall hangings to use.

For walls that are painted, your choice is almost unlimited. You can use a wall mural, a grouping of pictures, plates, plaques, and a clock. For large areas of neutral colors such as paneling, brick, or tile, accent them with wall hangings of vibrant, clear colors—a panel of fabric or a rug from Mexico in vivid colors, or an assortment of shiny copper molds and cooking utensils. On the other hand, when kitchen walls are covered with a colorful patterned wall covering, the wall hangings should be of neutral tones—copper, brass, wood, or wrought iron. If you want to use pottery or enameled items, key them to colors in the covering.

Good ideas to use: A bulletin board that is decorative as well as useful can take its place as a wall hanging in your kitchen. Or, try your hand at creating your own wall hangings. Frame several of your favorite recipes or your children's artwork, and mount them on the wall in an interesting fashion.

The compact Pullman-style kitchen above becomes a traffic-stopper by means of a wall mural showing a 1930 automobile. This one is executed in copper, but it's also available in wallpaper and vinyl-coated wall covering. The elongated lines of the car seem to enlarge the wall. This way-out wall treatment also helps define the central work area of the kitchen. The lengthy countertop can double as a buffet server when the occasion demands. Lighting sometimes can pose a problem in a Pullman kitchen. Here, fluorescent tubes behind a plastic grille provide plenty of nonglare illumination.

DISPLAYING KITCHEN TOOLS, POTS AND PANS

In addition to adding individuality to your kitchen decor by displaying your kitchen tools, pots and pans, you'll have the added advantage of having large, bulky utensils only at arm's length away, instead of almost inaccessible at the rear of a cabinet.

If you've recently become a gourmaniac, you'll like a ceiling rack for your custom pans—the omelet skillet, Chinese wok, and paella pan. You can hang the ceiling rack above a butcher's block, over an island work space, or above the breakfast table. Or, you can have racks on the wall, or above the range where utensils can hang from meat hooks within easy reach. Pegboard can also be mounted on the wall for smaller kitchen tools and gadgets. Open shelves offer another possibility for display.

The kitchen below is shy on cabinets, so the gourmet cook and chef hang their cookware on the walls. When they travel, they buy more kitchen tools and gadgets, and decorative accessories to add to their collection. This is a sure way to banish the bland look that often creeps into kitchens. The pots of greenery, and the breathtaking view beyond the full length windows visually expand the size of the small kitchen.

The antique clock placed above the home office area in the kitchen above is clearly visible from both the food preparation center and the dining area. Cook books, displayed on a shelf above the desk, are easy to reach.

Here's a kitchen decorator clock that also has a calendar on its face. It has a walnut-finished case with a white dial with brown numerals and minute markers. It runs with a battery-powered transistor movement.

Wall-mount racks that hold cutlery where it is convenient to the work space area. If these are to hold sharp knives, be sure that they are out of reach of small children.

Whether your utensils are of copper, aluminum, or have a glossy baked-on enamel finish, they will take on added charm when they are displayed conspicuously in a kitchen.

KITCHEN CLOCKS

Time flies, especially when you are working in the kitchen, so it is especially important that you have a clock that is clearly visible from the work area. From ancient sundials to modern electronic timepieces, clocks have made a larger contribution than merely recording the passing of time. Properly chosen, they bring a changing accent of beauty to a room. No wonder, then, that clocks through the ages have been carefully selected accessories.

Whether you want an old-fashioned key-wound kitchen clock that sends out a friendly tick-tock, or one that is electric-or battery-powered, you will find a large assortment of designs, colors, and sizes from which to choose—there's one just right for you.

There are Early American clocks inspired by the school clocks of years ago, ones of copper with an old-fashioned teakettle design, and antique wood-tone finish models shaped like an old breadbox or sugar box. There are contemporary timepieces with stylized designs in bold decorator colors, and also traditional types that are reproductions of all the well-known classic styles.

FAMILY HEIRLOOMS AND COLLECTIONS

In order for the kitchen to be a room that the entire family can enjoy, it must be decorated with the personal touch. And, what better way is there to give it a stamp of individuality than by using family heirlooms and collections as a theme for accessories.

Those of you who have inherited a set, or even a few pieces of old Staffordshire ware, Oriental china, Dresden, Sevres, or fine English porcelain are indeed fortunate. Get them out and display them on open shelves, or within a glass-doored cabinet where you can enjoy their beauty every day without the hazards of accidental breakage. Perhaps a few pieces of cut glass, sandwich glass, or pressed glass have been handed down to you. Even if you have just a creamer and sugar bowl, a compote, and a plate or two, arrange them in an interesting grouping and show them off with pride.

When possible, plan your kitchen colors and decorating scheme around these family treasures. Do the same if you have a collection of pewter, copper, brass, or cast iron cookware.

A cherished collection of Meissen ware was the inspiration for the new look in the remodeled kitchen below. In the eating area, a Java-stained hutch is mounted on the wall to hold an assortment of handsome pieces. A plate rail was built into the kitchen area to hold plates and platters where they can be seen and enjoyed every day. And, to emphasize the beauty of the rare collection, Meissen ware-patterned wallpaper is used throughout the room.

In the functional kitchen above, a collection of cast iron bakeware adds drama to the corner baking center. Included also are drawers that hold cookie sheets, cake and pie tins, and a butcher's block that rests under one end of the counter when it is not in use. Making use of collectibles, ceramic containers on the counter and on open shelves above hold baking ingredients, and old-fashioned candy jars also hold staples. The ideas in this kitchen are good examples of how you can use collectibles to add decoration and function.

There is apparently nothing under the sun that people do not collect—all the way from rare and expensive classic cars to seashells. But to many people, the most rewarding of all their collections are the ones they can display in their homes. A collection adds warmth, charm, color, and beauty to almost any room in the home, but especially so in the kitchen where so many hours are spent in food planning and preparation, and cleaning up.

Collections for the kitchen are all but limitless, and you can keep adding to them as long as you wish. In a country kitchen, display a collection of old keys hanging on hooks on the wall, a grouping of antique wooden spoons and spatulas, or an assortment of old cookie cutters. If you have a traditional style of kitchen, display a collection of glassware, figurines, plates, or spoons. In a contemporary kitchen, show off a collection of colored glass bottles, handmade ceramic bowls and pitchers, or a grouping of abstract wall hangings. However, for any style of kitchen, copper, brass, and pewter collections are a pleasing complement.

In the kitchen at the right, the cooking center is separated from the dining area with painted plank shelves suspended from chains that are hooked to the ceiling. Displayed on these hanging shelves are enameled cookware, ceramic and wooden serving pieces, and pots of thriving green ivy, all arranged in an artistic fashion.

The full-length window that lets in all of the natural light and a spectacular view of lush greenery outside is fitted with a series of three-inch-deep window shelves. They hold an extensive collection of seashells, small rocks, bits of coral, and gnarled pieces of driftwood. These were gathered a piece at a time, and represent the painstaking efforts of a series of beachcombing trips.

Besides the fact that the hanging shelves provide an ideal location for bright and colorful kitchen accessories, they serve to divide the space between the eating and cooking areas without obscuring the view outside from either of the two. The combination of natural and handcrafted items enhances the indoor-outdoor atmosphere that prevails.

FRUITS, VEGETABLES, AND GREENERY

The kitchen becomes a happier place in which to work when it contains some of nature's own handiwork. Fruits, vegetables, and greenery are yet another tool for the home decorator to use creatively, and they seldom require the same amount of investment as most other kitchen furnishings and decorative accessories.

Keep a wooden, ceramic, or brass bowl filled with fruit on the kitchen counter, on an open shelf, or on the breakfast table. Change the colors as often as you wish—from a bowl of shiny red or yellow apples to one of oranges, green or purple grapes, yellow bananas or pears, purple plums, or green limes. Or, combine several varieties and colors. For a change of pace, at Christmas you can fill the bowl with mixed nuts and a nutcracker. At Easter time, fill it with decorated or colored eggs.

Vegetables, too, can be a decorative accent. This is especially true during the harvest season when tomatoes, green and red peppers, squash, cabbage, cauliflower, eggplant, parsnips, and turnips are plentiful. Arrange several vegetables in a bowl, and place them where you can enjoy their color and form. In the fall of the year substitute a few ears of gold and brown Indian corn in combination with several sizes, shapes, and colors of gourds.

Plants, both green and flowering, will sparkle when they are set in the showcase of your kitchen windows. The natural light will make the colors of bloom and foliage more vibrant and glowing. A wide windowsill is an ideal spot for a window garden, or several glass shelves installed in the window. Or you may prefer to have hanging baskets of plants suspended from the ceiling.

The most successful window garden, regardless of whether it includes one or a number of plants, is one that is planned to suit the plants that it features in respect to light, temperature, and humidity. If you have a south window, grow a variety of flowering plants. East and west windows, too, get enough sun to satisfy some of the most attractive varieties of foliage plants as well as a number of flowering varieties. As a general rule, avoid placing plants in windows with a north exposure.

In a window garden that features a number of different plants, prepare for it by installing shallow plant trays of waterproof metal or plastic. Fill the trays to a depth of an inch or more with pebbles. After making sure that all clay pots that are visible are scrubbed and clean, you're ready to place your plants on display. Since all excess water can drain off into the pebbles beneath the pots, and add humidity to the air, watering chores are minimized and the problems of overwatering are resolved.

For a hanging garden effect, use pots with attached saucers that allow for drainage, or use metal or ceramic containers that will prevent water damage to the kitchen's furnishings.

If you don't have a windowsill that will accommodate one or more houseplants, simply supply a substitute by building a shelf supported by brackets. You can also put shelves across any part of the window. For these higher shelves, glass or plexiglass are

In the kitchen above, a collection of mugs brightens the backsplash area above the cabinet counter. Note how the mugs hang on a hat rack which has been extended to its full length. This attractive and functional idea provides for instant hospitality whenever unexpected guests arrive.

Viewed from across the room, the lines of the icon corn dryer below emphasize the slanting walls and long, narrow windows of bold architecture. The contrast between the display of the old coffee grinder and bean pots along with colorful new cookware is a decorating technique you may like.

70

The vivid bulletin board at the right is a quick and easy project to make. Cut a single carpet square into three rectangles for note pad, calendar, reminders, and messages. The carpet pieces, yarn borders, and tin pencil holder are all glued and tacked in place on a precut pressboard plaque that measures 14x18 inches.

In the kitchen below, watermelons, sketched, painted, and sculptured, add a note of whimsy and personality. Look for different types of paintings on wood, and other brighteners that will add interest to your backsplash.

good materials. Because of their see-through feature, they will not obstruct the view outside. For those who have a windowless kitchen, display your plants on open shelves hung on the wall and move them where they will get natural light a few hours each day.

If you are a devotee of gourmet cookery, grow an herb garden in your kitchen instead of the traditional houseplants. This will be decorative and, at the same time, provide an assortment of flavorful accents to add to your favorite foods.

Just because you live in an apartment, you don't necessarily have to lose touch with nature. Even if your kitchen is small, and you have room for only one small plant, don't be disheartened. It's still a touch of living green. Just keep in mind that green plants are easier to grow in apartments than the flowering varieties, which require strong light.

For apartment kitchens that are windowless, simply move the plants to a room where they will get good, bright sunlight for several hours each day. Remember that a plant in a small pot may need watering two or three times a week, while a large one needs watering only once a week. Water the plants you have in glazed pots less often than those that are planted in clay, porous types. Allow the surface of the soil to dry before rewatering them. If you're away from your apartment for a week or so, water your plants and set them back out of the bright light, then drop plastic bags over them. This will keep them alive for up to two weeks.

A few examples of plants that will grow in apartments are: sanseveria, bromeliads, dieffenbachia, philodendron, dracena, cactus, fern, ivy, peperomia, succulents, fatshedera, and syngonium.

CREATIVE KITCHEN CRAFTS

New craft techniques are continually being developed, and new designs keep creeping up that use already popular techniques. Here are how-to instructions for five unusual kitchen decorations—bulletin board (page 70), plaque made from children's salt dough, machine-made appliqué, still life painted on canvas, plus a very successful method for pressing vegetables (all on pages 72 and 73).

Kitchen bulletin board. Either cut or buy a precut pressboard plaque 14x18 inches. Sand it lightly and paint it with yellow acrylic paint. Then divide a 12-inch outdoor carpet square into three sections: one 8¾x12 inches, one 3¼x7 inches, and one 3¼x5 inches. Cut these with a clipping knife and glue into position. Glue on pink acrylic yarn to conceal the edges of the carpet.

For the pencil holder, paint an empty adhesive bandage can with orange lacquer and tack it in place. Decorate it with flowers and circles cut from self-adhesive plastic adhered to the tin and the board itself. Position a small notebook and calendar with tacks; attach a picture hanger to the back of the bulletin board.

Salt-bread dough plaques. To make the salt bread dough, combine two cups of flour, ½ cup of salt, and ¾ cup of water and knead with hands after mixing. If the dough is too stiff, add a little more water gradually. Roll out the dough about the thickness of piecrust, and cut it into whatever shapes you choose. Cookie cutters, small bowls, or glasses can be used to cut the

In the kitchen above, houseplants thrive in charming ceramic pots placed on top of the kitchen cabinets. They get natural light each day from the skylight and benefit from the artificial light, too. A refrigerator-freezer is below the plant grouping.

Items on the open shelves in the kitchen at the left can be picked out as they are needed. In addition to houseplants and a collection of decorative accessories, there is ample room for the homemaker to store her cook books conveniently.

72

outside shapes. The smaller pieces are cut out with a knife, or you can cut off pieces from the cookie cutter mold. Dampen both of the pieces of dough just slightly when sticking them together. The wall hanger is one from a Christmas tree ornament. Bake the plaques in a 350-degree oven for one hour. Allow them to cool, then paint them with acrylic paint. Use a final coating of a liquid plastic finish to preserve the plaques and make them easy to clean.

Artichoke wall hanging. Cut out the pieces of fabric from scraps of material that are coordinated by color. Use a related background fabric and cut it 26x21 inches, allowing a two-inch hem at the top, a one-inch hem at the bottom, and a ½-inch hem at each side. A heavy upholstery weight fabric (or decorator fabric sample) is good to use as background material. Pin the petals of the artichoke in position and zigzag them in place, using a satin stitch on your sewing machine. If you use a contrasting color of thread, it will separate the colors. Also, use a contrasting thread for stitching the words. Finish the hem, and slide a narrow brass curtain rod through the hem at the top. Hang it on the wall with a colorful cord fastened to each end of the curtain rod.

In the photo above, child's play becomes an asset. Salt-dough bread that children love to fashion into snaky coils and unidentifiable sculpture can also make whimsical sun faces (or other designs) to decorate the kitchen walls. You bake only the best and paint it to preserve it.

The patchwork artichoke at the right utilizes snippets of material too small for even a quilting bee. Simply cut out the petals and position them; then use a zigzag stitch on your sewing machine for a quick appliqué and clever cording.

You can use a whimsical approach to decorate an ordinary refrigerator door. In the photo at left, a piece of artist's canvas was fastened to the refrigerator door with rubber cement. Then, a still life depicting all the owner's favorite foods was painted on the canvas. Whenever a change is desired, the canvas can be peeled off.

The vegetable plaques below are the real thing. Thin slices of firm-textured vegetables are pressed and dried for three or four weeks, then artfully arranged and adhered to plaques. This project takes some time, but the result is unique kitchen art.

Still life canvas. See what a touch of homegrown art can do for an ordinary refrigerator door. Fasten a piece of canvas to the refrigerator door with rubber cement (for easy peel-off), and paint a still life on it that depicts a well-stocked refrigerator. The same method can be used for whatever design you choose.

Pressed vegetables plaques. First, remove the foliage from firm-meated vegetables such as carrots, eggplants, cauliflowers, beets, or mushrooms. Using a very sharp knife, cut center slices about ⅛ inch thick from them. Place the slices between paper towels for about an hour to blot up the moisture. Then arrange them without overlapping between pads of newspapers. Cover these pads with a board weighted with bricks or other heavy objects. Press the foliage separately in large books, or under a weight. Every two days for a week or ten days, remove the damp newspapers and replace them with dry ones to prevent mildew; then allow the materials to dry undisturbed for a minimum of two weeks.

Cut the plaques from plywood, pressed hardboard, or balsa shingles in the size and shape you want. Tint them with washes of acrylic paints and allow them to dry. Spread a thin coat of glue on the backs of the vegetables and press them onto the plaques. Place them under a light weight until the glue is dry. Paint the entire plaque with a coat of matte acrylic medium. Next, arrange the leaves and smooth them down to eliminate air bubbles. Allow them to dry before brushing them with three or four coats of matte acrylic medium. Dried vegetables may be left their natural colors, or the colors can be intensified with very thin washes of acrylic paints before applying the final sealer coats of medium.

chapter 4

KITCHEN FURNITURE

Because an eating area in or near the kitchen is one of the most popular family gathering spots in a home, it is important for you to select kitchen furniture that makes the area attractive and functional. How you furnish the area will depend on certain factors—the style of your kitchen, the size and shape of the space available, the mood you desire, the 'life-style' of your family, and the number of persons who will use it.

For your kitchen dining area, choose from breakfast sets or small-scaled dining room furniture, or stools for breakfast counters in both modern and traditional styles. They may be constructed of wood, plastic, or metal, or a combination of any of these materials with glass, vinyl, leather, or fabric.

Kitchen furniture is not confined to the eating area alone. If there is space for a small home office near the kitchen, install a desk, and hang some bookshelves above the desk to hold your collection of cook books. If yours is a large, family-style, country kitchen, you will probably want to include a comfortable rocking chair for relaxing moments, and a lamp for reading.

A warm and friendly atmosphere prevails in this charming dining area. Notice how the sliding glass door to the sun porch beyond adds spaciousness. Dining tabletop has a special finish for greater durability, and the chair pads are treated for soil and stain resistance.

BUYING KITCHEN FURNITURE

The message is mix in the informal family dining area below, with each piece of furniture serving a particular function or decorative need. The graceful curves of the bentwood chairs pair most attractively with the geometric lines of the Parsons-type dining table at modest cost to the owner. The mellow wood tones of the table, chairs, paneling, and island peninsula add warmth to the atmosphere as do the copper pitcher, ladles, and pots that hang in collected order above the island divider and the fireplace when logs are aglow. The antique clock, candle sconces, and cascading plant define the striking mantelpiece. And the baskets and vacation-collected paraphernalia further enhance the prevailing feeling of friendliness.

In planning a kitchen-dining area furniture arrangement that is appropriate for your family's needs, keep in mind the amount of space that is available and the general atmosphere, or degree of formality, that you seek to create, plus the size of your family.

DINING SETS, AND TABLES AND CHAIRS

Before buying any furniture, determine what can fit in your kitchen. For a grouping of average-size table and chairs, allow six and one-half by eight or nine feet of floor space. This much floor space will allow a clearance of 30 to 36 inches around the entire kitchen furniture grouping. This simplifies seating and serving.

Then, decide on the style of furniture that harmonizes best with your kitchen decor. For a formal feeling, choose a dining set of fine furniture wood in a traditional, country, or contemporary style. Many of the tabletops are treated with a special finish that is resistant to abrasions or stains—or both, and are thus practical for everyday use. Or select ornate wrought iron chairs and a glass-topped table for an elegant look. Equally formal, but with

An eating bar built onto an island peninsula can save you countless steps. The depth of such a counter should be 15 to 18 inches—24 if it is to be used for regular meals. Generally, a counter height of 29 inches is right for chairs, while 40 inches is needed for high stools. When a baby's high chair is to be slipped under the edge of the counter, the height should be approximately 32 inches (used with adjustable stools).

A table with built-in benches is ideal where space must be conserved. Since no walk-around space is necessary, an area 5¼ feet wide and a little less than 4 feet deep would allow for a table 28 inches wide and ample elbowroom for four persons. The addition of a narrow shelf would provide handy parking space for serving dishes, toaster, and coffee maker, or could be used more for decorative purposes as shown here.

contemporary styling, are the dining sets of rigid molded plastic, or ones of shiny chrome or brass with glass or see-through plastic tabletops, and chairs either of all metal or with upholstered backs and seats. Some of these materials may not be a practical choice for families which have small children.

A less formal approach might be a wiser choice when there are children in the home. Consider Early American styles, refinished dining sets, tables and chairs of rattan or bamboo, or tables with tops of plastic laminate material accompanied by vinyl upholstered metal chairs. They are serviceable and very easy to care for.

An inexpensive solution to the kitchen dining problem is a picnic-type table with benches, which accommodates a maximum number of persons in less space than that required for a table and chair grouping. Paint the picnic table a bright color with the benches to match or contrast. Or paint slats of each in different colors. Or paint the table white and perk it up with bright flowers or other stylized motifs cut from solid colors of adhesive-backed wall covering material. Let your imagination be your guide.

Finally, do not let limited funds put a crimp in your style. Watch for furniture sales, which generally occur in February and August. Do some window shopping a few days or a week prior to the actual sale, as some stores offer a reduction on merchandise before the ad appears. With the wide choice of dining furniture that manufacturers offer today, it is possible to select from all the major furniture styles in whatever price range your budget allows.

BUILT-IN COUNTERS AND NOOKS

If seating arrangements for two to four persons is all you need, an eating bar, more commonly called a snack counter, might be ideal for you. Children, especially, enjoy eating counter-style. A bar built onto a kitchen peninsula divider or against a wall of the kitchen or adjacent family room can double as an accessible eating space and as a serving counter when entertaining.

While snack bars may seem informal, they can be turned into sophisticated eating nooks by using fancy brackets to support the counter and by furnishing decorative chairs or stools. An ornamental strip can be used across the front edge of the counter, too.

A breakfast nook with built-in benches and table is still another practical suggestion for kitchen dining. This arrangement is good for those who have to conserve space, as a built-in nook eliminates the need for the usual walk-around space.

The colors and patterns you choose to accent your dining area will play a key role in creating the mood that is right for you. Don't be afraid to think big or to be daring, but use colors that harmonize with the style of furniture you have selected.

Modestly priced, bold-colored plastic table and stools (above) take up little space while providing an appealing snack center, especially for children. Durable yet lightweight, the snack set is practical for outdoor use, or parts can substitute as bar stools, TV tables, a telephone stand, or they can be disassembled and used for planters or ice buckets. Shown with the snack set are a pitcher and stackable mugs from a plastic dinnerware collection of neoclassic design, also very much in the modern mode.

In the setting at the right a warm, homespun feeling was inexpensively achieved by teaming rattan chairs with an old table newly accessorized with paint and ingenuity to complement the bright provincial wallpaper background. Wall shelves store crockery and kitchen molds, which add to the overall convivial atmosphere.

Here's a very attractive and practical dining arrangement for the budget-conscious and young-at-heart couple, especially if storage space is at a premium in their living quarters. The table is actually a slab door set on two bases of wallpaper-covered cardboard clothes hampers, thus providing dining space plus storage for out-of-season clothes or bedding all wrapped up in one. The hampers cost about a dollar and a half at the dry cleaners. The inexpensive bentwood style armchairs were painted a contrasting color.

An old-fashioned treadle sewing machine base discovered in a junk shop sparked the idea for this striking, yet practical dining table. You can do the same with a similar base. Apply two coats of fire-engine-red paint—the same color as that on the wall—and purchase a butcher's block top. Screw the two together from under the block top. Then, add interest to the table with black wrought iron director's chairs with vinyl covering.

DO-IT-YOURSELF FURNITURE

Unfinished furniture is relatively inexpensive to buy, and it costs very little to paint, stain, or antique. However, the variety of designs that are available is somewhat limited.

Used furniture, on the other hand, offers many possibilities. You can either refinish it, or dismantle it and rebuild it, using new materials to replace portions that are no longer serviceable.

Check antique shops, thrift shops, and junk shops for furniture pieces, taking your imagination right along with you. For example, a door added to the base of an old table or narrow cabinet can be transformed into a handsome dining table with paint, stain, and/or vinyl-coated wallpaper or one of the adhesive-backed wall covering materials. If you want a circular table, hunt for a pedestal base, have a sheet of ¾-inch plywood cut to whatever size you desire, and mount it on the pedestal. Paint, stain, or antique the entire table the color and finish of your choice.

Family hand-me-downs sometimes offer hidden possibilities. An ordinary round lamp table with no distinctive design features can be painted or antiqued and outfitted with a large glass top that increases its diameter so that four can be seated comfortably for dinner. Finish chairs to match, and add cushions covered with brightly colored soil-resistant fabric, or vinyl. If one of the family members is handy with tools, you can stretch dollars by building your own dining accommodations in the form of a bench and table or a snack counter. Detailed plans for easy, do-it-yourself furniture projects are offered through several of the women's and home improvement magazines, or at many home building supply and paint supply stores.

chapter 5

KITCHEN APPLIANCES

Today's household appliances have made kitchen drudgery a thing of the past. If they are chosen wisely and properly cared for, they will provide you with many years of convenient, dependable service.

Because your major appliances—range, refrigerator, and dishwasher—represent a considerable investment, evaluate all of the features before you make a choice. If you buy the wrong one, the mistake will be difficult to live with. It may be costly, too.

No one model is best for every family, and with so many models and features to choose from, it is easy to become confused. So, before making a purchase, read articles in newspapers and magazines, and talk with friends. Do some comparison shopping, checking the warranty and service offered. The best buy for you is the appliance that meets your family's present and future needs, the space you have, and, of course, your budget.

Small appliances offer additional convenience, but no family has the need, money, or space for every labor-saving appliance available. Here again, consider your family's needs; buy only those that will be used often.

Where you live and the space available determine, in part, what appliances best suit your needs. Portable dishwasher with work top is a good choice for this efficiency kitchen. Wall niche provides space for speedy electronic cooking and for blender and mixer.

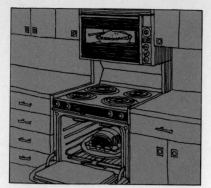

Split-level range — two ovens

Eye-level model — high oven

Built-in surface unit teams...

...with separate ovens

CHOOSING LARGE APPLIANCES

Today, major appliances offer more quality and convenience at less cost than in years past. Nonetheless, they represent a large investment. Become familiar with different models, and shop wisely.

Ranges — styles, construction, and features. The first basic consideration in selecting a range is the type of fuel you'll use — electricity or gas. If you are building a new home, your choice may be determined by fuel costs in the area in which you live or by what you are used to. If you are remodeling, the availability of a gas line or 220-volt service may be the deciding factor.

1. Freestanding models are finished on both sides, as well as on the front. The units contain an oven, broiler, and generally four surface elements. Although freestanding styles are lower in cost and offer flexibility in arrangement, the trend has been more toward the built-in look achieved by other styles.

Double-oven, split-level models are freestanding units that look built in. In some makes, this style is a combination microwave (see top of opposite page) and conventional range.

2. Drop-in, slide-in, and eye-level models of single oven ranges, which have a built-in appearance, are available, too. These models are positioned in a kitchen counter between base cabinets. The slide-in style is a variation of the freestanding range, with a broiler or storage drawer beneath the oven. The drop-in model sits on a base that generally matches the cabinets.

3. The conventional built-in range — a counter cooking surface separate from the oven — offers the convenience of suiting the oven height to the homemaker. Or, an oven/broiler combination can be installed in a wall and used with a separate counter cooking surface. However, installation costs are higher and the units cannot be moved. Also, this arrangement requires more wall space.

4. Glass-ceramic top ranges have heating elements sealed under the glass-ceramic top, and each of the four heating elements has its own thermostatic control. There are no exposed burners or coils, and the entire cooking surface can be wiped clean easily.

For service and durability, look for a range with an exterior finish of stain-resistant porcelain enamel, stainless steel, chrome, or pyroceram. Controls should be easy to read and to adjust. The handles and knobs should be made of heat-resistant material.

Ovens that self-clean or have easy-clean features (see page 124) are designed to save time and energy. Other convenience features include temperature-controlled surface units or burners; oven controls to keep food at serving temperatures or to change oven temperature during the various stages of cooking; surface griddles; rotisserie attachments; meat thermometers; oven door windows; electric clocks; appliance outlets; and storage drawers. For added safety, there is lighting for the range top and oven and indicator lights to show when the heat is on. You can choose from several colors or decorator trim kits, and design your own range front.

Electronic ovens. Microwave ovens are rapidly increasing in popularity. The reason is simple. Microwave cookery is fast and, thus, highly adaptable to today's homemaker's busy schedules.

In microwave ovens, a vacuum tube, called a magnetron, converts electricity into microwave energy that is absorbed by foods and liquids in the oven. This energy, in turn, penetrates the food from all sides, setting the food molecules in motion. It is this vibration that generates heat inside the food and cooks it. Contrary to earlier misunderstanding, microwave ovens do not emit ionizing radiation that is detrimental to human beings.

There are two basic types of microwave ovens—portable or countertop ovens, most of which operate on standard 115-volt household current, and the larger, freestanding or built-in models which operate on 120-240 or 236-240 current. Some of these larger units are equipped to cook electronically, conventionally, or both ways at the same time. Some are two-oven models, incorporating a separate conventional oven with a microwave oven.

Refrigerators—styles, construction, and features. Generally speaking, there are two basic types of refrigerators for home use—the conventional model, with a single, exterior door, and the combination refrigerator-freezer with two doors.

1. Conventional refrigerators are designed for the storage of fresh food. They will not store food for long periods or freeze food. However, a built-in evaporator unit maintains a temperature adequate for storage of frozen foods for one or two weeks.

2. Combination refrigerator-freezers have separate refrigerator and freezer sections. These sections may be either one on top of the other or side by side. Both, however, are designed to store fresh and frozen foods for long periods.

Look for an outside finish of porcelain or baked enamel and a seamless construction. Also look for linings of porcelain enamel or of another rust-resistant material. The shelves also should be rust-resistant, and preferably adjustable. Check for a tight-fitting door and sturdy hinges. Find out whether or not the insulation is moisture-resistant, odorless, and indestructible.

Time- and energy-saving features include nonfrosting or automatic defrosting operation and an automatic ice cube maker or dispenser. For convenience, there are right- or left-hand door openings; foot pedal openers; magnetic door closing devices; door shelves; and slide-out, swing-out, or roll-out shelves. A five-year warranty on compressor units, seasonal control, and special storage areas add to economical, efficient operation. Decorator colors and a trim kit to do with as you wish add extra eye appeal.

Waste compactors. The waste compactor is a major home appliance that greatly reduces the bulk of trash by compacting bottles, cans, plastic containers, and paper under force. It has won acceptance because it keeps the kitchen cleaner and neater, and because it results in less clutter and fewer unsightly trash cans. It operates on a 120-volt, 15 amp-fused standard household circuit, and it fits in a standard 15-inch kitchen base cabinet space.

Microwave oven

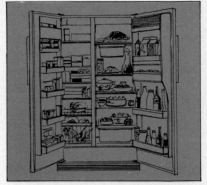

Side-by-side refrigerator

Top-freezer refrigerator

Waste compactor

Disposer

Built-in dishwasher

Under-sink dishwasher

Portable dishwasher

Sinks. While they are not actually appliances, sinks are included here because they generally are the most used piece of kitchen equipment and are essential to food preparation.

Sinks are available, both rimmed and rimless, in various sizes and finishes, and with a single-, double-, or triple-bowl. Triple-bowl models include a separate, small bowl that will accommodate a disposer. With a dishwasher, a single bowl is ample.

For durability, choose either a stainless finish or porcelain enamel, which comes in several decorator colors and white.

Food waste disposers. Waste disposers conveniently dispose of much of the wet waste that accumulates in a kitchen. They accomplish this by hammering, cutting, grinding, shredding, and pulverizing the waste as it is being washed down the drain.

The batch-feed type is first filled with food waste, then covered. The continuous-feed type allows food to be added during the grinding process. Both types are activated by a switch.

In buying a disposer, choose a sturdy one, preferably with a ½ hp. motor. For efficiency, there should be an overload protector switch, an automatic reversing switch, a dishwasher drain guard baffle, and a rind positioner. Also look for an impeller liner to absorb noise. Corrosive-resistant materials throughout the unit and a positive-pressure water seal contribute to the durability.

Styles of dishwashers. If you are building a new home or remodeling the kitchen you now have, a built-in dishwasher will likely be your preference. The front-loading, built-in models fit into a 24-inch base cabinet space. An exception is the type that fits underneath the sink. The front-loading convertible models, however, can be built in at a later time, if desired. The portable or convertible styles are designed for families who cannot, or who do not wish to, install the appliance permanently.

Construction and features of dishwashers. The exterior finish should be of stainless steel, copper, brushed chrome, or porcelain enamel. Look for an interior finish of porcelain enamel or another acid-resistant finish. They also should provide flexibility for convenience in loading. The controls should be conveniently located and clearly marked. All of the newer dishwasher models have improved wash systems over the earlier models.

Different models of dishwashers vary in the length of the wash cycle and in the number of cycles available. Plan ahead and select the model that will meet the changing needs of your family. In addition to the regular wash cycles, there are cycles to prewash or prerinse; rinse and hold; a wash-only cycle; a heavy-duty cycle; a sani-cycle; and a heat-only cycle, the latter for use in warming clean dishes before serving a meal.

Other special features include flexible loading racks for odd-shaped utensils and dishes, an automatic detergent dispenser, and an automatic wetting agent injector to prevent spotting and to speed drying. For safety, look for a motor overload protector, a water overflow protector, and a safety switch. Decorator front panels and a do-it-yourself trim kit are available with most models.

CHOOSING SMALL APPLIANCES

Small appliances can be extremely useful, but do be selective when you consider buying them. Choose those that you will use often. Check the warranty to become familiar with its conditions. After purchase, fill out and return the warranty card—promptly.

Toasters. There are basically two kinds. The most common type is the well or upright toaster, with two- or four-slice capacity. For large families, the four-slice is perhaps the better choice. Look for models with two controls if preferences for degree of brownness vary. With either size, models with wide wells can toast English muffins, waffles, and toaster pastries, as well as bread.

Oven-type toasters have a horizontal rack. Use them for any breads handled by the uprights, plus open-faced sandwiches. You also can bake potatoes, biscuits, and frozen pies in them.

Broilers. Most table broilers do more than just broil. This is especially true of the horizontal broilers, which may be round or rectangular in shape. Some have thermostats and can be used for heating casseroles, frozen dinners, coffee cakes, and pies. Removable grills are included with some. Some may be used with a rotisserie spit or a shish kabob attachment. Smoking and spattering are eliminated through a specially designed drip pan. Another type, the vertical broiler, operates just like a toaster. It has two heating elements that broil both sides of the food at the same time. The interior rack is adjustable to accommodate bacon slices or varying thicknesses of food.

Electric knives. These make the task of carving hot or cold meats easier and more efficient. They also slice brick ice cream and cakes without mashing. You even can use them for shredding lettuce and cabbage, and for slicing fruit, vegetables and cheese.

Electric knives have two scalloped-edge blades that move back and forth, resulting in a shearing action. All you have to do is guide them. In addition, they rarely, if ever, need sharpening.

Your choice is basically between the plug-in models or the cordless styles. Some, however, can be used either way. Look for a comfortable handle, tight-fitting blades of high-carbon chromium stainless steel, and easy blade release and reassembling. Also, be sure there is a convenient on-off switch, safety lock, grease guard, and a built-in table rest or a facsimile.

Mixers. These can whip, beat, stir, cream, mix, and blend ingredients far better and easier than by hand. Portable models have become increasingly popular because they are inexpensive and take up little space. Portable styles are especially handy for light-duty and general mixing tasks. Some come equipped with a stand.

While most standard mixers have a removable motor head, they are heavier, and, thus, somewhat less convenient for hand-held mixing jobs. One big plus for standard mixers is that they free both hands during mixing. They also excel for heavy-duty or long mixing tasks. Portables have 3 to 12 speeds; standard models, 10 to 14.

Toaster

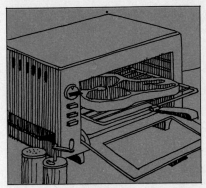

Broiler

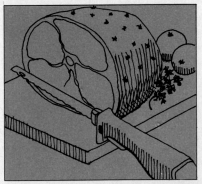

Electric knife

Portable mixer

Blender

Coffee maker

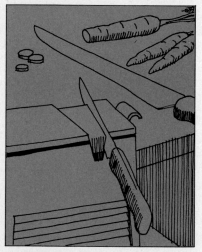

Electric knife sharpener

Blenders. Here is an appliance that rates high on the popularity poll. And small wonder! It can chop, puree, pulverize, crumb, and grate an incredible variety of foods. A blender can homogenize ingredients for salad dressings, sauces, and gravies, and make dips and desserts. Some can be used to crush ice (with water).

A blender is not designed to replace a food grinder or a mixer. Rather, it is a nice addition to either or both. You should not use it to grind meat or to extract juices from fruits or vegetables. Nor should you use it to whip egg whites, mash potatoes, or mix heavy doughs. However, it can be used for light batters.

Blenders consist of a base unit that houses the motor, a cutting unit or blade, a heat-resistant glass or shatterproof plastic container, and a cover. The controls may be push-button, rotary, or the slide/switch type. Some have solid-state circuitry.

Look for ease of cleaning separate parts and for a container with convenient handle, pouring lip, and legible markings. The unit should be adequately weighted so it does not creep or tip during operation. For safety, an instant on/off control is important.

Coffee maker. Freshly brewed coffee without any fuss or bother is the convenience that lends charm to coffee makers. You may choose between percolator, drip, or vacuum types. With each, performance is best when the coffee maker is used to its capacity. Thus, you should select a size that provides the number of servings you need most often. For small families, those of two- to three-cup capacity are popular. Larger families might choose a coffee maker with a capacity of from 9 to 18 cups.

Look for a comfortable handle of heat-resistant material. The construction of the coffee maker itself should be of a design and material that is easy to clean. There are coffee makers of stainless steel, of aluminum with a porcelain finish in decorator colors or a chrome-plated finish, and of glass with stainless steel parts. An increasing number of coffee makers are completely immersible.

The spout should be dripproof and free of crevices. Cup markings should be readable. Other nice-to-have features are a signal light, flavor selector, and reheat setting. Also, it is very helpful to have a see-through coffee level gauge.

Can openers. You might want to consider a model that is multipurpose rather than one that opens cans only. Some open bottles and jars, and some sharpen knives or a combination of knives and scissors or pencils. Other openers may be in combination with an ice crusher, juicer, shredder/slicer, or an electric clock. Usually, they are countertop models, but some are wall-hung.

There are both automatic and semiautomatic openers. With semiautomatic models, the actual cutting operation is automatic, but something must be held down. Automatic openers remove the lid and hold the can in place after the unit shuts off.

The cutting devices used are of two types. One is a cutting wheel that rotates freely, so no portion of the wheel gets more wear than any other. This is a slight advantage over the stationary blade type. With the latter, the can is rotated around against the blade, and the same point of the blade is used over and over again. This type, however, does handle cans with corners more easily.

In shopping for a can opener, look for sturdiness and stability. Also look for a design that opens all shapes and sizes of cans. (Tall cans require more space between the countertop and cutting device.) The cutting assembly should be easy to remove for cleaning, unless the opener is a model that opens cans just below the rim. With this type, the cutting device stays clean because it doesn't cut into the lid and come in contact with any food.

Frypans. In these you can fry, stew, braise, roast, bake, and sometimes broil. In short, they are highly versatile. Rectangular- and square-shaped frypans are the most popular, but round ones are also available. They are made of a variety of materials and finishes, and are attractively designed for use in serving as well as for cooking. Teflon interiors are gaining in acceptance, although stainless steel and aluminum are also used. One model, made of glass ceramic rests on an electric heating base. Some have shallow bases and deep lids. Others have deeper bases to accommodate large roasts and fowl. Sometimes, a bake rack is included. One has a warming tray beneath the frying surface.

Immersibility is important, so look for removable heat controls that make this possible. This control also should be easy to remove. In addition, the thermostatic control should be easy to read and to use. Check to see that handles and feet are resistant to heat and that there is adequate space between handles and pan to prevent burns on fingers. Some other features you might find handy are an adjustable, tilting lid and and adjustable tilting of the pan itself. Also helpful is a signal light to indicate when the set temperature has been reached. Choose a size based on your needs. The 13- or 15-inch models are a good choice for large families, while a smaller family might find an 11- or 12-inch size ample.

Ice crushers. For families who do a lot of entertaining, or who like things festive for themselves, an ice crusher can be a real joy. Several are multipurpose. One, for example, is a combination can opener/ice crusher. Another is a combination crusher/drink mixer that can perform a variety of whipping and blending tasks. In some nonelectric as well as electric models, you have a choice of fine or coarse crushing. Some dispense the ice into an attractive serving tray. Both electric and nonelectric models crush ice easier and faster than by the arm and mallet method.

Multiappliance centers. Several manufacturers offer power units from which a number of small appliances can operate as attachments. Some of these units can be installed in a countertop or on a wall. One is designed to be built into an 18-inch kitchen base cabinet. This same unit also is available as a self-contained console cabinet. The cabinet provides space for both using and storing the various attachments. Some of the most popular attachments for these centers are a blender, mixer, ice crusher, juicer, meat grinder, coffee mill, knife and scissors sharpener, salad slicer/shredder, can opener, and cooking stirrer.

Can opener

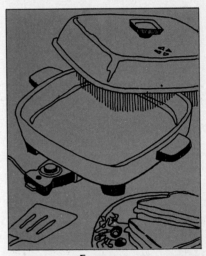
Frypan

Ice crusher

chapter 6

KITCHEN STORAGE

Finding a place for everything and keeping it there, in reasonably collected order, is one of the greatest challenges a homemaker faces. The many processes connected with preparing and serving meals call for an astounding number of kitchen gadgets, utensils, and dinnerware. And each item needs to be stored.

There are numerous ways to store these items—some are simple, others are rather ingenious. Some special storage units can be custom-built by a carpenter or a handy husband. Others are designed by kitchen cabinet manufacturers who offer a wide selection of accessory units that utilize cabinet space to the best advantage, as well as add to working convenience.

There are also many inexpensive devices available to help you get organized and stay that way. Some can even expand the space you have to a surprising degree.

The following pages contain a potpourri of kitchen storage ideas that will help you meet the challenge. Explore them diligently, and make use of the ones that will help you solve some of the special storage problems you find yourself up against.

This innovative concept offers convenience, economy, and abundant storage. The 5x7-foot kitchen core contains sink, refrigerator, freezer, microwave oven, waste compactor, dishwasher, and serving cart. Cordless utensils plug into thermostatically controlled receptacles.

ORGANIZING STORAGE SPACE

Storage that is well designed and well organized makes any kitchen a joy to work in. To make the best use of existing storage space, place equipment and food within easy reach of the work center at which they will be used. Exceptions to this are surplus canned goods bought in quantities and utensils, tools, and items that are used for entertaining—serving pieces, china, and silver.

While it is important to have enough cabinets, it is even more important that the cabinets themselves are designed both for practical use of space and for convenience in removing and returning supplies. To achieve these objectives, you can do one of three things: **1.** You can have units custom-built and added to your present cabinets; **2.** You can build the units yourself; or **3.** You can purchase one of the many specialized built-in units offered by cabinet manufacturers.

On the other hand, if you don't have the time or money to do any of the above, replace the stationary shelves with adjustable ones. Half shelves and step shelves, too, add convenience and space, as do the portable organizers described on pages 94-95.

Shallow, slide-out trays (above) provide maximum storage space for canned goods and make each can easily accessible. You can see at a glance the exact contents of each shelf. When outfitting a cabinet in this way, allow more space between the trays at the bottom for larger-sized cans. A closet can be turned into a canned goods dispenser in a similar way, but with stationary shelving. All it takes is plywood shelves set at an angle, with lower side of shelf at the front. Add facing strips of 1x2's to hold the cans steady. When one is removed, another slides into its place.

Pullout storage drawers (right) for dinnerware, cookware, or appliances, can be adapted easily to whatever space you have. Begin by dismantling an existing cabinet interior. Use ¾-inch plywood to make twin sets of bifold cabinet doors, which are held together with piano hinges. Make the drawers with ½-inch plywood, banded by 1x4 hardwood. To support drawers mount heavy-duty, telescoping drawer slides onto cabinet sides.

Use the following guide to help you organize your kitchen equipment and supplies for greater overall convenience. (Since the mixing center is sometimes close to the refrigerator-freezer and at other times is adjacent to the range, the storage suggestions for this particular area have been treated separately.)

Near the sink: 1. Utensils, tools, and supplies that are first used with water, and those that are used in the clean-up process are most handily stored near the sink. **2.** Plan cabinet space for dried foods, canned soups and shellfish, teakettle, double boiler, saucepans and lids, colander, strainers, and chopping board—if portable. **3.** Allow space for coffee maker, too, unless you have an electric model and prefer to keep it on the counter. **4.** You will need space for detergents, scouring powder, floor cleaner, polishes, all-purpose cleaners, and possibly ammonia and bleach. (If youngsters are around, plan locked or out-of-reach storage for these.) These items can be stored in cabinets or on the counter. **5.** Provide divided drawer storage for cutlery, brushes, scrapers, sponges, towels, dishcloths, and aprons. **6.** Plan space also for a trash container if you don't have a trash compactor, and a dish drainer and tray if you don't have a dishwasher.

Near the refrigerator-freezer: Here, you will likely prepare beverages, lunchboxes and/or sandwiches, and salads. **1.** Cabinet space is desirable for the supplies and utensils associated with each, for canned goods to be chilled before use, and for refrigerator dishes. **2.** This area is good also for storing wrap products needed, tape, and markers. **3.** Also allow space for a can opener and small tools necessary for preparation of the foods mentioned.

Near the range: 1. Pull-out shelves or drawers are a real convenience for the heavier cookware you will use at the range. These include frying pans, griddles, saucepans, and covers. **2.** Plan cabinets to hold canned goods, spaghetti and other pastas, non-condensed soups, and seasonings. **3.** If foods will be dished up here, you'll also need space for serving dishes, platters, and some dinnerware. **4.** Drawers can accommodate small tools, tongs, cooking spatulas, serving spoons and ladles, hot pads, thermometers, and duplicates of mixing and measuring spoons.

Near where you mix: This area is most commonly close to the refrigerator, but it may be near the range. In either case, provide additional space to store the following items. **1.** In the cabinets, you need space for shortenings, sugar, flour, salt, baking powder, vinegar, spices, cake and other mixes; also, bowls and casserole dishes, some of the larger baking utensils, and your mixer. **2.** For the shallower utensils—cookie sheets, cake and pizza pans, and muffin tins—plan vertical divided storage for greater convenience. **3.** Provide drawer space for mixing tools: rubber spatulas, mixing spoons, pastry brush, blender, rolling pin, cookie cutters, and flour sifter—if drawer is deep enough or sifter is small. Since this is the area where there is generally the widest variety of sizes and shapes of supplies and utensils, it is the one where you can especially benefit from planning storage space.

The lazy-Susan principle, generally used to make full use of corner space, can be applied to standard base cabinets as well. This ingenious whirl-around unit makes even deep storage shelves readily accessible.

The photo above shows side with 7-inch-deep shelves for canned and bottled items. Shelves are adjustable to accommodate various sizes of cans. At a touch, the unit swivels to reveal half-circle shelves (below), holding an assortment of frequently used appliances. Width of the semicircular shelves is 33 inches.

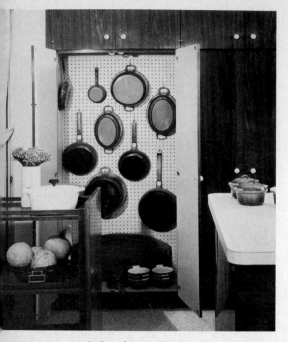

Only a few inches of clearance depth are needed to hold pans, skillets, and lids. Mount them on hooks attached to a panel of perforated hardboard, as shown above. If you prefer to conceal the cookware, convert the area into a shallow utensil pantry. Build a box around the area and hang plywood doors across the front.

A good place to store bulky pans and elusive lids is on the inside of a pantry door, as seen in the photo at the right. Mount perforated hardboard to a frame of beveled furring strips, leaving an inch or two all the way around to permit the door to close properly. Use ½-inch thick, triangularly shaped boards for the side pieces of the two lid racks at the bottom. Lower racks should protrude 3½ inches; upper racks, 2 inches. Nail 1½-inch wide slats horizontally. Trim interior shelves slightly to allow for depth of utensils and lid rack.

USING PEGBOARD

The development of perforated hardboard was undoubtedly one of the biggest boons ever for the cause of storage. Teamed with a myriad of specially designed hooks, it can hold an astonishing variety of kitchen tools and utensils. Use it on the inside or backs of cupboard or closet doors. With it you can turn waste space into usable storage space and hang utensils so they are easy to find and are easily accessible. And, it costs very little.

Types and sizes of perforated hardboard. There are several kinds of perforated hardboard, usually ⅛ or ½ inch thick. The most popular type is dark brown in color. It can be painted whatever color you desire. Some kinds are available in other colors. Perforated hardboard comes in various sheet sizes, the most common being 4x8 foot. You can also have the panels cut to the size or sizes you need at most building supply stores.

Also available are perforated panels of plastic that have adhesive-backed strips for easy installation. All you have to do is peel off the backing and press them in place. These come in yellow, green, orange, or white. With a matching shelf, they provide an expanded work wall. One is shown at the top of page 105.

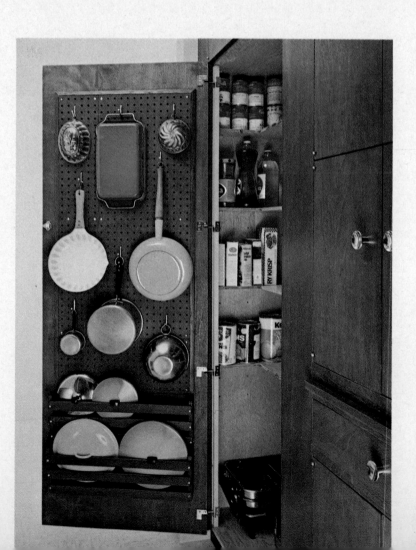

The compact baking center at the left is actually a big plywood box. The back and sides are fitted with perforated hardboard. This holds utensils and tools out of the way, but makes them easily accessible. Adjustable shelves provide versatility of storage for larger, odd-shaped bakeware. There is also a pull-out work board to supplement counter space. The baking center is equipped with heavy casters, which make the unit easy to move.

Special preparation tools are easy to find and get at on the handy hang-up below. It slides out on a center-mounted drawer-glide at the bottom. Hooks may be moved or new ones added at any time. A narrow-door base cabinet can be converted quite easily. First, remove the hinges and attach a drawerlike box near the base. Then, slip a perforated hardboard panel into a vertical saw kerf that has been cut on the inside of the door. Attach a drawer pull at the center.

Working with perforated hardboard. If you have a good set of tools, you can cut your own perforated panels. All you need is a power saw or a handsaw, some sandpaper, a plane, a rasp, and a wax or colored pencil to use for marking the panels.

If you're cutting the hardboard with a power saw, use a low-set blade with just two or three teeth showing. Hold the board down with the flat of your hand and work with the smooth side up. If you're working with a hand saw, select a fairly fine-toothed saw (8 to 12 points per inch) and cut the panel, bending the hardboard slightly to overcome saw 'buckle.'

After the hardboard is cut to size, smooth the edges. With grainless hardboard, use a rasp, stroking it lengthwise. For all other hardboard, use a shallow-set plane, holding the plane at a slight angle so that the shearing cut is downward from the surface of the board. This method will prevent fuzziness.

For round or beveled edges, use an ordinary plane. For jobs where the beveling is extensive, use a bevel plane, and adjust the plane to the bevel you need. If you have lots of rounding to do, cut a bevel along the edge, then sandpaper it into a rounded edge.

Hardboard tends to fuzz up slightly under sanding, especially standard-grade board. Control this by applying a washcoat of shellac before final dressing. Don't sand the surface of the panel.

USING PORTABLE ORGANIZERS

One quick and inexpensive way to get your cabinets organized is to use portable storage organizers. They are easy to install or to remove—some are freestanding, others need to be screwed down. They are adaptable to many sizes, shapes, and types of cabinets. Thus, they are especially practical for apartment dwellers, families on the move, or people who anticipate a move or two before being able to settle down permanently in a home of their own.

Portable storage organizers generally are made of plastic or have a steel wire frame covered with a washable, cushion-coating. All of them are designed to make stored foods, utensils, kitchen tools, cleaning supplies, and wrap products more easily accessible, or to provide more efficient use of the storage space at hand.

If your cabinets are crowded or seem constantly in a state of disorder, take a look at these inexpensive items. They are easy to find at many hardware, variety, and department stores.

This caddy (above) has a compartment for storing cleaning supplies, and a built-in bar for dishcloth and towel. Attach it to the inside of the door below the sink.

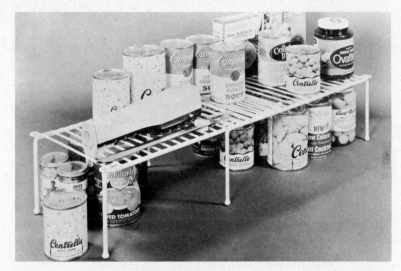

This shelf unit (at right, above) is especially useful for food cabinets without adjustable shelves. Units can be used separately or stacked, to double or triple the interior space, yet they provide easy access to each row. Unit extends from 18 to 32 inches. It also can be used right-angle fashion in corner cabinets.

This rack (at right, below) is one of several types used for organizing and holding a complete dinnerware service for eight. Plate rack holds up to eight each of different sizes. Cup racks hold up to 12 cups.

Six different types of organizers are shown on these pages. Some others that are available are mentioned under the accompanying photos. In addition, there are holders designed to attach to the inside of cabinet or closet doors for glasses, cups, cookware and/or lids, and rubber gloves. There are also caddies to hold an iron and ironing board, and one for vacuum cleaner tool attachments.

Racks are available to hold pots and pans, pot lids, ice cube trays, and platters. There is one to hold a desk-style telephone, with space below for a phone book, and one that stores wrap products, nested-fashion, in a minimum of space.

Make order out of chaos in your kitchen drawers, too, with special drawer organizers. Use trays with built-in dividers or the separate, different-sized dividers that interlock to fit the space within. Both types reduce clutter, and they may prevent an unnecessary accident by letting you store sharp, pointed tools and cutlery apart from the everyday flatware.

These handy, pullout bins (above) fit in base cabinets for storage of vegetables, and some fruits if you wish. The wire types are more commonly available as accessory units from cabinet manufacturers, but you can also buy plastic bins that are easy to install, or stackable units that just sit on the base of the cabinet.

This firm-footed accessory shelf (at left, above) allows for two-tier stacking of assorted sizes of jars, tins, and wrapped foods in your refrigerator. The washable, cushion-coated unit, slightly more than 5 inches high, 5 inches deep, and a little under 11 inches long, can be used on cabinet shelves, too.

This double-row rack (at left, below) fastens to the inside of cabinet doors, and keeps spices handy and orderly. You can also store spices in a shallow unit that attaches to the underside of a wall cabinet—or on turntables that rest on a shelf. There is even a sliding type that holds spice cans to underside of shelf.

ADDING PERMANENT STORAGE

Extra storage space often can be gained by installing cabinets or portable units in open floor areas. Peninsulas, dividers, and wall cabinets added in space that is going to waste are all devices that can be used for adding storage space. Another way to gain space is to use the space between the countertops and cabinets.

PENINSULAS

A peninsula is an extension of a work counter or a row of cabinets. Often, a peninsula is used to bridge the gap between two work areas—the preparation of food on one side, and the serving of food on the other. It also performs a double duty by providing extra storage space below and additional counter work space.

Some peninsulas include a drop-in or built-in cook-top range, a dishwasher, or even a sink. With one or more of these items so conveniently located, you will save both time and energy. For example, with a dishwasher installed underneath the peninsula,

Pictured below is an attractive dining setting that has abundant storage space—an ideal solution for short-on-space homes or apartments. Open cubes are stacked on modular units for a wide wall of storage. Graduated, woven baskets are perched atop cubes for even more storage space. You can change the arrangement, add to it, or dismantle it and take it with you if you move. All components adapt readily to new surroundings.

The table and chairs are arranged to provide the recommended clearance of 30 inches all the way around.

This round dining counter (at left) sweeps around the end of the kitchen peninsula. Its top drops down six inches from the counter work surface to accommodate the standard height chairs. In keeping with the light, airy look of the rest of the area, the suspended storage unit above the peninsula is equipped with glass doors on both sides. The eating bar can double as a buffet counter when you are serving outdoor parties on the deck of the adjoining family room.

In the photo below, an island unit with built-in cooking elements and serving counter extends to include an informal dining bar. Attractive, petal-shaped lighting fixtures are suspended overhead to provide incandescent light for evening snack times.

you can simply remove the dishes, flatware, and crystal from the dining area and transfer them directly to the dishwasher. If the peninsula also serves as a snack or breakfast counter, this location for the dishwasher will save even more steps.

If the peninsula serves as a cooking-serving divider between the kitchen and dining areas, and has a drop-in range or built-in cook-top range, why not consider adding a narrow shelf five or six inches above the surface? This arrangement will permit you to serve food from the cooking side and to remove it from the other.

Some peninsulas have cabinets above the countertop as well as below. This type of installation yields maximum storage facilities and acts as a partition to distinctly divide two areas.

A peninsula also can be used strictly as an informal dining bar, with stools that can be tucked underneath when not in use. Or it can be used as a desk unit, with a convenient place for cook books, household records, a telephone, and a TV and/or radio.

If you do not have the floor space in your kitchen for a full-fledged peninsula divider, there are numerous alternatives that will serve as a substitute. You can place a storage cabinet, a desk, or a portable cart at right angles to the end of a row of cabinets, or you can devise a hinged work shelf that can flip up when you need additional countertop surface. Still another way to create a small peninsula is by using slide-out panels just below a regular countertop. Regardless of the way that you choose to create a peninsula in your kitchen, rest assured that you are putting otherwise wasted floor space to very good use.

Every detail of the kitchen at the right was planned to save steps. A center work island is positioned for easy access to the sink, refrigerator, counter cooking surface, and the ovens, each located in good working relationship to one another. Ample counter surface was planned adjacent to both the cook top and the ovens. Storage for glasses and dinnerware is near the dining room— a real step-saver. Tall shelves at the bottom of the cabinet (not visible in the photo) make room for party servers, punch bowls, and other less frequently used entertaining utensils.

The six-sided island below has a sleek look, and it is functional—it opens up all around to become a versatile storage compartment. Cooking utensils have special drawers and racks. Two extra surface burners supplement the main cook top.

ISLANDS

An island may be any size and shape, depending on your special needs and available space. It can be square, rectangular, L-shaped, U-shaped, hexagonal, or circular. It can have built-in appliances on one or two sides, with work surfaces on the perimeter and a center-mounted lazy-Susan to bring small items within reach.

Many islands are almost a kitchen in themselves, containing a range, dishwasher, under-counter refrigerator, and a sink. With this type make sure that a wall oven and refrigerator-freezer are close to specialized storage and work centers. When the island has a built-in range, it must have a vent hood and a counter surface for preparing and serving food. Some are simple units that are suitable for families who like to barbecue year-round. They must have a grill and a hood. Others may be used simply as a table or a bar for informal family dining.

If a small island is all you need, or all that space permits, a rectangular or square unit will yield the most work space. Consider including knee space along one side if a dining area isn't provided elsewhere in the kitchen. This will enable the unit to double as a snack counter. If you need additional storage space, stand two narrow cabinets back to back. Top them with a maple chop block for a special salad and meat preparation center. Or, if making candy is your specialty, use marble for the surface. If the island is fairly small, consider putting it on large, global casters. Presto, you have a portable unit. You might even like to install electrical outlets and a cord for serving convenience.

When planning any island arrangement, be sure to allow at least three feet of clearance between the island and work areas.

ADDING A WALL OF STORAGE

In small kitchens, or in dining areas or family rooms, the utilization of unusued wall space will add immeasurable storage space as well as convenience. Units can be built-in or freestanding.

There are factory-built modular units available that you can arrange yourself in whatever combination best fits your needs. Most commonly, these wall units include a combination of doors, drawers, and open shelves. While the open shelves offer convenient, low-cost storage, they present more of a cleaning problem. At the same time, they enable you to display some of your favorite decorative items. Whether open, closed, or a combination, adding wall storage helps you use valuable space.

If you have special storage needs, custom-build the unit yourself. This is easy if there is a handyman in your family. You can obtain project plans from home and family service and building publications, and from building supply dealers. These plans can be adapted to your own requirements.

If a lack of storage space is your problem, the kitchen pictured below is an idea worthy of duplication, especially for an apartment or a small home. Eye appeal, versatility, and fingertip convenience highlight the storage/work wall. For a cook who likes to see everything at a glance, the open shelves provide a decorative, yet accessible place for frequently used seasonings, staples, and tableware. Cook books store handily, a short reach away from the mixing center, and the toaster has a separate niche to the left. Note the proximity of the dishwasher to the dining area.

Extra storage can be gained in surprising places. A false front under a counter cooking surface, and often in front of a sink, lends itself to a tilt-out storage niche as shown above. Remove the false front and add a bottom and a back of ½-inch plywood. Insert a 2x2-inch wooden peg at each end to prevent drawer from falling too far forward. Use this space for spices and small tools.

Organize miscellaneous kitchen items in a storage cabinet attached to the underside of a wall cabinet. Make it as long as the upper cabinets and approximately ten inches high by eight inches deep. Use 1x8s with 1x2 facing strips at each end and middle. To duplicate this cabinet (right), insert ¼-inch hardboard dividers on the left side, and a one-inch dowel for paper towels at right. Hinge 1x8 doors to shelf, and attach door chains to the facing strips. Use wood putty on joints where new and old cabinets meet, sand, and stain or paint the unit as desired. For tips on working with hardboard, see page 91.

ADDING CABINETS IN WASTE SPACE

You can squeeze extra storage space into kitchens and adjacent areas by adding cabinets in otherwise wasted space.

Between counters and upper cabinets. Midway cabinets offer fingertip convenience for numerous small items while utilizing the wasted space between a counter and a wall cabinet. Although these cabinets are not difficult to build (see instructions below, photo at left) you can purchase ready-made ones, which are available from several kitchen cabinet manufacturers. Some of these have lights built into them to provide localized light for the work counter. There are also portable drawer and cabinet units with tilt-down doors that are easy to install.

Along walls. Often it is possible to add a standard wall cabinet under a window or along a passageway that is not too narrow. These cabinets average 12 to 13 inches in depth and come in a number of heights. A 36-inch high cabinet would also gain added countertop work space, which always comes in handy. If a cabinet depth of 12 to 13 inches will crowd things too much, consider using a shallow, tall cabinet—even four or five inches. This is often sufficient to accommodate a variety of canned goods, paper products, tools, and utensils that are not too bulky. If possible, provide for adjustability of shelving so that the space can be used to maximum advantage. Be sure to brace cabinets well for stability.

When storage space is at a premium, and you own your own home, put the space between wall studs to good use. Even though this space is shallow, it will hold glasses, cups, and small tins.

In corners. In cabinets that turn corners, install lazy Susan-type units to make full use of space. (See page 91.)

The areas shown here were once an outdated kitchen, an antiquated laundry, and an unheated porch. There's no lazy space in any of them. In the laundry above, each child has three hooks for jackets and playclothes. Mittens and sports equipment are kept below the counter on the left. The stainless steel sink serves triple duty for laundry, after-play cleanup, and flower arranging. Laundry supplies and vases are stored in the cabinets above the appliances.

The children's favorite corner is the food and beverage center (at left, above). Everything they need for between-meal snacks is concentrated in one area. The under-counter refrigerator in the center holds all the soft drinks and snack items.

The planning desk (at left, below) is used mainly as a telephone center. It is also a handy place for storing cook books and for menu planning.

The white stained cabinets throughout the room camouflage fingerprints, and the easy-care vinyl-coated wall covering with lively floral motifs lifts everyone's spirits.

Adjacent to this area are the newly remodeled kitchen and dining niche.

The base cabinet above, close to the food preparation area, keeps portable appliances all together and each one handy when needed. Shelves should be adjustable to provide for both short and tall appliances, and for future changing needs. Appliances also can be stored conveniently on a lazy-Susan unit of a base cabinet (see page 91). Concealed storage for appliances keeps them clean without constant dusting and polishing.

Small appliances store handily in a niche with tambour front door (at right). With the door down, appliances are neatly hidden. When the door is rolled up, they're ready to go to work. You can make tambour doors like this with thin strips of wood, such as screen molding. For flexibility, glue strips to a firm canvas backing. Finish with paint or stain, and install under wall cabinets. If niche has no exterior counter surface, a fold-down door with heavy-duty hinges, plus chains or desk brackets would provide a sturdy work counter for kitchen chores.

STORAGE FOR SPECIAL EQUIPMENT

Kitchen equipment such as small appliances, seldom-used cookware, and items for entertaining, plus canned and packaged foods and those staples that are purchased in large quantities should all be stored where they are readily accessible. This takes some thoughtful planning, but it can be accomplished.

SMALL APPLIANCES

Make portable appliances work for you, not hinder you. Store them where they are accessible—not in some seldom-used place where you will have to hunt for them.

The best place is on a counter, if you have generous work space in your kitchen—for a can opener, mixer, blender, frypan, and broiler-oven. The best places for a toaster, are close to the area where you store bread, butter, and jellies or where you eat, whereas a coffee maker is handiest placed near the sink. If space is limited, store appliances in the handiest spot possible.

Do not operate the coffee maker—or any appliance—close by the sink. A cord might slip, or you might handle the appliance with wet hands—both are safety hazards. If several appliances are used at once, be sure the wiring is ample to accommodate all of them. Usually only one heating appliance can be used on a general-purpose circuit at one time.

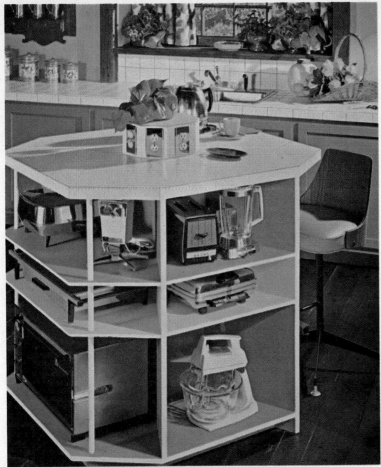

The tall, narrow cabinet above has adjustable shelves for convenient storage of small appliances. Available ready-made, these cabinets are 20 to 24 inches deep and can accommodate many appliances.

You can build an appliance island like the one at left above, to hold all your small appliances. In just an instant, you can move any of them up to the counter surface for use. The outlets surrounding the top pedestal permit use of several appliances at the same time. (For detailed instructions, order Project Plan No. 3607-2 from Reader Service, 1716 Locust Street, Des Moines, Iowa 50336.)

The appliance nook at left, below is built to rest on a snack bar. It holds toaster, condiments, and other necessities close at hand when needed, out of sight when not. Make a plywood box with sliding doors to fit the amount of space you have.

If space permits, a baking center like the one above is ideal for storing roasters, casseroles, and other awkward pans. The 24-inch wide, below-counter area files large pans on edge, and the casseroles upright on pull-out shelves. Make both slide-out shelves and dividers from ¼-inch hardboard. (For tips on working with hardboard, see page 93.)

The centrally located kitchen at the right was planned for practical use of space and fast food preparation. Diversified storage includes components that can be interchanged to fit future needs. Everyday staples and frequently used utensils store within easy reach of the maple work counter. Cook books, trays, platters, casseroles, and pans store edgewise on upper shelves. Hardboard dividers fit rabbeted grooves. Note the panel of soffit lighting that is above the work counter surface.

STORAGE FOR SELDOM-USED COOKWARE

In addition to the numerous tools and utensils that are used daily or weekly, the average home also contains a number of items that, while useful, are needed only occasionally. These, too, require space, yet they don't need to be stored right at your fingertips. It makes better sense not to devote prime space to seldom-used equipment, especially if your kitchen storage space is limited.

Kinds of seldom-used equipment. Items that generally are needed only from time to time include: large mixing bowls, meat grinder, gelatin molds, cookie sheets, holiday cake tins and cookie cutters, large roasters, fondue pots, and utensils used for canning and freezing in large quantities. Depending upon family habits, the list might also include some small appliances that have been purchased or received as gifts, such as an ice crusher, corn popper, automatic juicer, ice cream freezer, and waffle baker.

Practical storage locations. Cabinet space that is high or hard to reach on a daily basis lends itself to storage of some of these seldom-used items. Shelves that are seven feet high or more are ideal for lightweight equipment. A cabinet over a refrigerator-freezer is also a good location, as it is usually recessed. The heavier and more bulky kitchen utensils and portable appliances are better stored at a lower height, even if this means storing them in a cabinet or in a closet, or, if necessary, on shelves that are away from the kitchen work area.

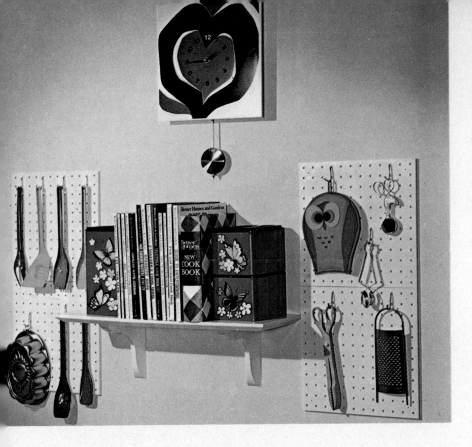

Find the cook book you need at a glance by storing your favorites on a shelf, preferably near the mixing center. At the left, cook books store on an 8x24-inch shelf as part of a wall unit that also holds tools and utensils within easy reach. The cordless wall clock reflects the character of the kitchen—the heart of the home.

The cook book shelf below has a pull-out easel that holds an open book within easy view. Build it of ¾-inch plywood, a couple of wood strips and a ¼-inch dowel as a stop for the easel. Fill nail holes with putty and paint, stain, or antique. Project plan also includes a desk organizer and cutting board. Order Project Plan No. 3811-1 from Reader Service, 1716 Locust Street, Des Moines, Iowa 50303.

STORAGE OF COOK BOOKS

Just as a doctor, lawyer, or architect needs special reference sources, the homemaker needs cook books. Whether you are a homemaker who loves to painstakingly prepare gourmet dishes, or one who prefers short-order style cookery, there are innumerable cook books to make it easier. In addition to general, all-purpose cook books, there are books devoted to fowl, ground beef, seafood, cheese, desserts, make-ahead meals, recipes and menus for entertaining—even eating and staying slim.

The amount of space you'll need for storing your cook books depends on how many you enjoy having access to. Plan convenient storage so that it is easy to locate and get at the one you want.

An ideal arrangement is to have a planning center with built-in shelves for cook books. This gives you a place to sit and relax while you browse through your cook books and plan your meals. Counter or shelf space near the mixing center is also a handy spot. And you might also use attractive bookends to hold them in place. You can buy an inexpensive study-stand or devise an angled holder on which to conveniently perch a book while you are preparing a recipe. A decorative-type easel holder designed primarily for holding pictures adapts well to some sizes of cook books.

If counter or cabinet space near the mixing center isn't available, a shelf on a nearby wall provides both accessible and decorative storage. Whatever you do, don't just keep your cook books tucked away in a drawer—visible storage is far handier.

Add interest to your dining area with a few wall-hung storage boxes (above) for dinnerware and bric-a-brac. For the cabinet frames, use 1x12 pine. For the shelf doors, use sidelights (windows made to flank an entry door). Attach doors to boxes with hinges, then add magnetic catch latches and a pull knob. Mount cabinets to the wall with a 1x2 strip nailed to the top inside corners. Drive screws through the nailer strip into your existing wall studs.

Plan dividers that do more. The trio of modular cabinets (at right) separates the living and dining areas while also creating some much needed storage space. Shelves, drawers, and vertical dividers inside the cabinets are custom-fitted to hold crystal, china, silver, and other serving items. The cabinets are made of plywood, with a semi-gloss white lacquer to give a furniturelike finish. On the living room side the cabinets provide hanging space for paintings and artwork. The units can be used separately, as shown, or bolted together for a full wall of storage.

STORAGE FOR ENTERTAINING NEEDS

Items used for entertaining often are special in one way or another. This is true regardless of whether they are expensive to replace, treasured family pieces that can't be replaced at any cost, or inexpensive items that are hard to find. Therefore, safety and accessibility are the main considerations here, whether you choose open shelves or closed cabinet storage.

Dinnerware and serving pieces. Store these items in a freestanding divider adjacent to the dining area, or convert a nearby closet into a party pantry. Custom-fit the pantry with shelves and drawers to provide convenient, safe storage. If you do a lot of entertaining, include space for a mobile cart to save steps. Except for cups, dinnerware lends itself to stacking, both for efficient use of space and for convenience in handling. Pullout drawer units eliminate unnecessary reaching and lifting.

Glassware and crystal. Shallow storage is best for these. Build shallow cabinets along a wall or between wall studs or use adjustable shelves. These reduce waste space—two inches of clearance above stored glasses is adequate for easy removal. If glassware must be stored on deep shelves, install half shelves or step shelves.

Odd-shaped pieces and other party items. Provide a shelf of 16-inch depth for flat storage of oversized items. Store trays and platters in vertical dividers or in shallow drawers. Also plan shallow drawers for tablecloths, place mats, napkins, ashtrays, candles (if not near heat), and a compartmented one for silver.

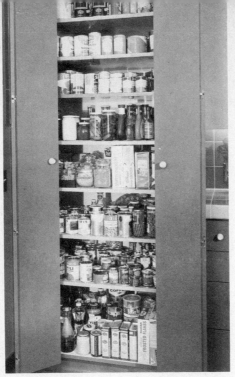

A one-time broom closet (far left) is now an efficient food pantry. Plastic trays on wire racks screwed to wood shelves slide out to bring each item within easy reach. Trays like the ones shown are available at many hardware, department, and variety stores.

Build a food pantry (near left) as wide as space allows. Use bifold doors if pantry is wide and passageway is narrow. The mortised hinges used for the doors here are completely concealed when the doors are shut. Make the shelves adjustable to accommodate a variety of sizes.

Obtain space for a shallow pantry (below) from a wall cavity or expendable doorway area. This one measures 6x3 feet, and it is 1 foot deep. Use plasterboard to make the pantry walls, then frame the opening with standard door molding. Next install U-shaped shelves of ¾-inch plywood, mounted on 1x2 supports. Add shelves of 1x2s and lath strips to the plywood door, and hinge to jamb. Cover outside of door with room-matching wallpaper.

STORAGE FOR FOOD SUPPLIES

The amount of space needed for storage of food supplies is determined largely by your shopping habits and by the size of your family. If you shop several times each week, a moderate amount of space will probably suffice. However, if you shop only once a week, or less frequently, you will need considerably more space. This is also true if you like to take advantage of sales on food items that you use frequently, and buy in large quantities.

Types of storage. Well-designed storage is especially important for food supplies so that it isn't necessary to remove a dozen items to find the one you want. A walk-in pantry with shallow, adjustable shelves is ideal, but few of today's homes can spare the space. Special pantry units are a good alternative. These provide well-organized storage and considerably relieve the load otherwise placed on the cabinets in the kitchen. A number of cabinet manufacturers have such units. Some units have double doors with versatile shelving built into the doors themselves. These open book-style to reveal additional shallow units, either stationary or movable, or a combination of both. Some units are less intricate, but all of them rate high on convenience and versatility.

If you want to build your own pantry units, there are project plans available through home and building publications, and home building suppliers. If these plans don't fill your needs, try removing fixed shelves from a cabinet and replacing them with pullout drawer-type ones. Or convert fixed, straight shelves to provide convenience by slanting the shelves slightly toward the front and by adding 1x2 facing strips to the front edge. All these ideas provide additional storage space for food supplies.

chapter 7

PROBLEM KITCHENS

An ideal kitchen has ample storage space, plenty of countertop area, a good traffic pattern, appliances that meet your family's needs, and a decor that makes the room a pleasant one in which to plan and prepare meals. Unfortunately, all of these desirable qualities are not always found in today's kitchens.

All too often the kitchen is too small with inadequate work space and storage facilities, or the kitchen's basic equipment is not arranged for maximum efficiency. Some kitchens do not have windows—this is true of a great many apartment kitchens—that let in natural light and a bit of cheer on a sunny day.

Another problem, although of a completely different nature, is that of adding a spark of individuality to look-alike kitchens—those that are mass-produced for the ever-increasing number of mobile and modular homes.

While there is no one easy answer to all these problems, there are numerous small solutions that can alleviate, if not eliminate, the biggest problems of each. Some are found on the following pages, others in the chapters on Kitchen Planning and Kitchen Storage.

A little inventiveness yielded around-the-clock convenience in this 6½x10-foot kitchen. Now, there's a refrigerator-freezer, a dishwasher, and a self-cleaning oven, plus ample work space. Light colors expand the space and the flower-bed wallpaper lifts attention to the ceiling.

Before this well-planned kitchen was revamped, even a simple meal required countless trips between the range and refrigerator on one wall and the sink and work counter on the other wall (see the Before plan below).

The door of the old refrigerator was left-hand hinged, opening inconveniently toward the hall. There was no countertop space adjacent to it on which to set foods either.

In addition, three people were a crowd around the table, and the only spot for the high chair between mealtimes was right in the line of traffic.

In the same exact space, a far more efficient kitchen evolved just by converting to an L-shaped plan. This permitted all the appliances, including a new dishwasher, to be consolidated within the L, freeing the former appliance wall for family meals.

Best of all, the new arrangement involved no costly alterations in plumbing or basic structure. The new snack counter can accommodate four people with elbowroom to spare—five if necessary. Between meals, it serves as a desk or as added work space for party preparation. Its height, 32 inches, allows the high chair to slide below, out of the way.

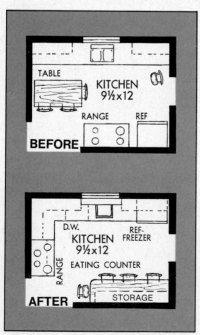

THE TOO-SMALL KITCHEN

Even if your kitchen is cramped, poorly arranged, and/or has little work or storage space, don't despair. Remodeling it into an efficient, more spacious work area may not be impossible after all. Perhaps just rearranging the kitchen equipment can produce a more workable and pleasant food preparation and serving center.

REORGANIZING IN THE SAME SPACE

Familiarize yourself with the different, efficient arrangements discussed in the chapter on Kitchen Planning. If the structure is sound, first try to work out a plan that doesn't involve making changes in the plumbing or basic structure. If a convenient arrangement can be provided without making these changes, so much the better. It will save labor and materials costs.

Actually, the replacement of older appliances with new ones can create a surprising amount of space. Today's refrigerators provide more refrigerator space in less floor area than older models. The popular 30-inch range styles can save up to 10 inches of space if you now have an older, wider model. If there is presently a wall and separate counter cook surface, you can consolidate both into 30 inches and acquire 18 inches or more additional counter surface. The new self-cleaning models take up no more space.

Perhaps you will gain as much as 24 inches if you install a built-in dishwasher. The virtues of these appliances are well known —they can cut your clean-up time about in half, plus help keep the kitchen cleaner and neater all day. There is also an under-the-sink model designed for the very compact kitchen. In addition, with a dishwasher a single-bowl sink, which takes up less space than the double-bowl style, is ample.

A trash container is a must in every kitchen, unless you have an automatic waste compactor. Above is a basket of nonmarring polyethylene with added practicality built in. Its hinged lid contains a deodorant block for freshness. Trash clutter is just a memory with this container. Teamed with the container are durable plastic bags for tear, tote, and toss disposal.

Numerous accessory items can add convenience to a kitchen, remodeled or otherwise. If space doesn't permit a built-in chopping block, countertop or pullout style, don't use the work counter. Instead, get a portable model for cutting, chopping, and slicing tasks. Shown at left is a board of glass ceramic material, which is durable and efficient. For greatest convenience, store portable chopping boards close to your sink or food preparation center.

PLANNING SPACE FOR MAXIMUM EFFICIENCY

Utilizing every nook and cranny can do wonders to expand storage and work space. With a dash of skillful planning, you can turn a small, short-on-everything kitchen into an efficient one.

First, take a look at the outer, or visible, space you have. If the space between the counter and the upper wall cabinets is not being used, you can add narrow cabinets in between. You can have them custom-built, or build them yourself, to resemble the midway cabinets shown on page 100. If these don't appeal to you, you can obtain factory-made ones from kitchen cabinet manufacturers. Some have built-in lighting for added convenience. Here's another idea for this space: install cabinet or drawer-type accessory units, which are available in housewares departments.

In passageways that aren't overly narrow, there are numerous ways to increase work and/or storage space. While concealed storage is often preferred from the standpoint of maintenance, consider using pegboard material (see pages 92-93). This comes in small or large panels, colored or unpainted, and can hold almost anything you can think of in the way of kitchen utensils. Narrow shelves and wall-hung units provide storage space as well as decoration. Many furniture stores carry attractive wall storage units. Some magazines offer project plans for building different kinds of shelves and cabinets yourself.

If you can spare six to nine inches of depth along a pass wall, you can build a tall, shallow pantry that will accommodate innumerable canned or boxed items, glasses, cups, and other small tableware. However, if you can spare up to 10 or 12 inches, the pantry will be so much more versatile. A tall, shallow cabinet needs to be braced during use, but it can be made removable.

A roll-out pantry is great for utilizing any leftover space between a refrigerator and a wall. The pullout storage unit rolls out on heavy-duty wheels. Make the back, top, and sides of the pantry from ¾-inch plywood; use ½-inch plywood for shelves. To steady and stop the unit, mount a drawer guide on the wall.

Accessible ingredients make any job easier, but the niche at right functions as more than just a storage area. Tiered shelves utilize every inch of space and keep spices in applepie order. On the bottom cabinet, the large chopping block doubles as a food preparation area and as a surface on which to carve large roasts or fowl. For rolling out pastry or candy, there's a pullout marble surface. It works like a drawer, yet takes only two inches of vertical space.

To convert an idle wall into a useful one, hang a unit that can function as added storage, work center, bar, or as a desk. The single-compartment style unit shown at left is 40 inches high, 24 inches wide, and 6¼ inches deep, with five adjustable shelves. For easy cleaning and durability, the work surface is of laminated plastic. The door, in decorator colors, rolls down to conceal the contents of the unit when you wish to do so.

Clean-up supplies and miscellaneous kitchen equipment are easy to find in the organized closet below. Normal closet depth of 24 inches allows for shelves of 12-inch depth, with room in front for stand-up items. For hanging-towel storage, install a one-inch diameter dowel between walls. Support shelves with 1x2 cleats nailed to the wall. Slanted shelf keeps folded paper bags neat and easy to reach.

Standard kitchen wall cabinets offer still another possibility for adding storage and work space in a small kitchen. They don't have to hang up high on the wall; they can stand low and provide you with both storage and counter or serving space at the same time. There are several heights available, but a 33- or 36-inch height would be a good choice for doing double duty.

If the pass wall is too narrow for cabinets of any depth, and you own your own home, you might build between the studs and provide space for shallow items such as spices, small canned or boxed goods, glasses, cups, or even the cookware lids. A built-in ironing board cabinet can be used in the same way. Fold-up shelves, attached to a wall at counter height, come in handy when extra work space is needed and the traffic can be temporarily discouraged for the occasion. A fold-down shelf might also be attached to the open end of a line of base cabinets for the times when additional work space would render you invaluable service.

Step shelves and half shelves will increase your storage space like magic, and adjustable shelves will provide versatility to meet your changing needs. Don't forget that the inside of cabinet and closet doors can utilize wasted space also (see pages 92, 94, and 107). Even the dead space in front of many sinks can be put to good use in a way similar to that shown on page 100. And if you have a corner cabinet, capitalize on it. Use lazy Susan-style cabinets or accessories for food storage in order to make otherwise hard-to-reach items readily accessible.

Opening up a quartet of cramped rooms yielded this attractive, workable, and airy kitchen (above). The bedroom, shown at left center in the Before plan, was moved to an unhandy breakfast room off one end of the original kitchen. Interior walls between the den, bedroom, kitchen, and butler's pantry were then removed to open up the area. This permitted an expanded work counter with refrigerator/freezer and a cooking island just a few steps away. In addition, space was gained for a roomy dining area, a built-in desk unit with shelves to house cook books and television, and a washer-dryer niche.

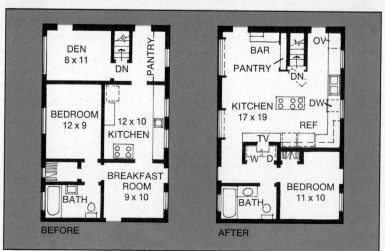

DEN
8 x 11

DN

PANTRY

BEDROOM
12 x 9

12 x 10
KITCHEN

BATH

BREAKFAST
ROOM
9 x 10

BEFORE

BAR

OV

PANTRY

DN.

KITCHEN
17 x 19

DW

REF

TV

W   D

BEDROOM
11 x 10

BATH

AFTER

The canned goods cabinet (left), handy to the cooking island, is 12 inches deep and actually doubles as a door to the basement. Heavy hinges allow it to swing out on casters. It rarely has to be moved, however, since the basement is used only for storage. Additional space for foods and kitchen goods is provided in the stationary tall cabinet around the corner on the left, as well as in cabinets along the generous work counter wall. Vent hood above the range top removes odors, grease, smoke, and heat, and it lights the cooking surface.

This entry from the dining room (below) was originally the butler's pantry. Although somewhat narrow because of the stairway to the basement on the right, enough space was gained for placement of the ovens on the near end of the extended work counter. Fluorescent tubes in the soffit provide general illumination. Tubes under the wall cabinets give supplementary light for the work surface.

COMBINING SMALL ROOMS

If your home consists of numerous small rooms, you might consider opening up two or more of them to provide space for a larger, more efficient kitchen. Often, you gain better use of existing floor area, and improve traffic flow as well, when you remove nonload-bearing interior walls, too. Expanding tiny rooms into a more spacious one generally costs less than would a new room addition. Sometimes, local building restrictions prevent expansion of the house itself, so consolidation may be the only solution.

Working with a multiroom floor plan is, of course, a bit more complicated than working with a scaled plan for one room only. It need not be overwhelming, however, if tackled properly.

Study the various types of good kitchen arrangements presented in the Kitchen Planning chapter. Decide which one would best suit your work habits and the needs of your family. You might have to make some compromises, but often opening up several small rooms allows more leeway for the plan of your choice.

Another advantage of combining two or more rooms is that it usually provides sufficient space for a combination kitchen-family room, which is so compatible with today's informal living style.

When you have some general ideas in mind, seek help from a kitchen planner. This type of remodeling is best handled by an expert, who will incorporate your ideas into a specific plan.

If you decide on a kitchen-family room, include a divider of some type—a work center, or a serving or dining peninsula. While openness makes it easy to communicate with family members, a separation of some kind between the work and recreation areas tends to afford the cook more privacy while she is working.

THE WINDOWLESS KITCHEN

Sure! Being able to see the outside world now and then, especially on a beautiful day, makes lighter work of kitchen duty. But, even if your kitchen is windowless, it needn't be dreary.

In windowless kitchens, it is very important to provide ample artificial light. It is needed not only for efficiency and safety, but it also makes the kitchen a more pleasant place in which to work. Good lighting is even more necessary if the appliances and/or cabinets are a dark color. If this is the case, use light colors for walls and floor when you redecorate. These will help reflect the artificial light and create a brighter kitchen.

Be sure you have good general lighting, too. Supplement it with localized light for the work centers. This lightens the overall area, and helps eliminate work shadows. For special lighting requirements and additional tips, see pages 120 and 121.

If there is a bare wall above the sink, you can decorate it with a large picture or with a group of small ones. Bric-a-brac or small plants on corner shelves attached to adjacent wall cabinets also add cheer. You might hang a mirror above the sink, so if the doorbell rings you can primp quickly. One mirror comes in a window-type frame to which curtains may be added, as shown below.

The kitchen above is typical of many windowless kitchens. Rising above, behind the sink, is a bare wall—hardly an inspiring view to confront numerous times every day. If you find yourself looking at a stark wall day in and day out, consider adding a bit of decoration. A poster, pretty hanging wall brackets, or other wall decor can spark up this work area and perk up your spirits—at little cost.

What a difference a little decoration can make. To the right is the same kitchen with a few small changes. Cabinet inserts have been covered with adhesive-backed vinyl-coated wall covering with a burlaplike texture. The most obvious and striking change was created by hanging a mirror-window. It adds brightness and spaciousness, and it has a window ledge on which to set small potted plants, if you wish.

THE MOBILE HOME KITCHEN

Mobile home kitchens don't need to look stereotyped. Even though mobile homes are mass-produced, dollar-for-dollar, they represent good value, and the materials used are generally of the easy-care type. All they need is a touch of individuality, which you can add.

When selecting dining furniture, keep in mind that it must be of a size and scale suitable for the eating area. There are scaled-down versions of all popular furniture styles in whatever material you choose—wood, metal, plastic, or a combination of two or more. Add colorful table appointments and cookware that reflect your tastes. The use of unusual window treatments can contribute an individual note, too. For a coordinated effect, use the same fabric to cover seat cushions and to make a wall hanging. If you want to partition off the work area from the dining area, use a room divider or folding screen that is decorative as well as functional. Display your collectibles on shelves, or mount them on the walls. Some creative kitchen crafts would add a special touch and provide hours of enjoyment in the making. Browse through the chapter on Kitchen Decorating for other ideas.

While the mobile home kitchen generally rates high on convenience and low on maintenance, it presents a different sort of challenge than the average home. Because they are mass-produced, the kitchens tend to look alike. The real challenge lies in creating a note of individuality.

In the mobile home kitchen below, the scroll design of the wrought iron dining chairs and the colorful table appointments contribute a graceful note to the surroundings. Balls of fringe cascading along the bottom of the curtains add sparkle to the window areas. Canisters not only add a bright touch, they house staples close to the mix center. The chopping board, too, is handy, and it provides a bit of cheer to the corner.

Other ways to add a personal touch include a display of colorful cookware on the range and/or a collection of plates, spoons, keys, pictures, or creative craftwork for wall interest.

chapter 8

LIGHTING, WIRING, AND VENTILATION

While it may be necessary to make compromises when planning a new kitchen or remodeling an old one, it is not wise to skimp on lighting and wiring. Harsh light, or dim or poorly distributed light leads to eye fatigue and accidents. There are ways to avoid these lighting pitfalls with adequate planning.

Proper wiring is essential for safety and for appliances to give top-notch performance. It is time to update the wiring system if the radio fades, the TV picture shrinks, lights dim or flicker when appliances are turned on, appliances operate slowly, fuses blow, or the circuit breaker trips frequently. It is especially important if you have several appliances operating from the same outlet, or few outlets, requiring the use of extension cords.

Ventilation, too, is highly important. The removal of grease, smoke, odors, heat, and moisture that accompany cooking not only reduces the frequency for (plus cost of) cleaning walls, draperies, and furniture throughout the house, but makes the kitchen a more pleasant and healthful area in which to work.

Good kitchen lighting is dramatically illustrated here with luminous ceiling providing excellent background illumination, supplemented by localized light for each work area and for dining. Vent hood contains lights for cook center as well as fan for adequate ventilation.

The use of a light color scheme throughout this kitchen takes maximum advantage of both natural and artificial light. Ceiling panels yield excellent general illumination; lights built into range hood and recessed in upper cabinets complete the lighting system. If light for work surfaces cannot be recessed, brackets may be wall-mounted and fitted with a shielding device to prevent glare.

Below is a kitchen that is literally easy on the eyes. Lighting in the extended soffit and recessed under wall cabinets yields shadow-free work surfaces, warding off eye fatigue. Note also how the lighting accents the decor, highlights the cabinets and sink, and even adds texture, creating a warm, cheery atmosphere.

LIGHTING AND WIRING

Efficient kitchen lighting can be achieved only through a combination of general background illumination and localized lighting for each of the work centers and the eating area.

LIGHTING REQUIREMENTS

For the most efficient general lighting, a full or partial luminous ceiling is an ideal solution. However, ceiling fixtures or suspended luminous lighting fixtures are effective and moderate in cost. For a luminous ceiling or ceiling panels, use a minimum of one 40-watt fluorescent tube for each 12 square feet of floor space, or a 60-watt incandescent for every 4 square feet of panel. If a ceiling fixture is desired, plan 150 to 200 watts incandescent or 60 to 80 watts fluorescent for the average kitchen of 75 to 120 square feet. Or, use one or more suspended luminous ceiling fixtures, providing 2 watts incandescent or ¾ to 1 watt fluorescent for each square foot of the kitchen area.

Ceiling color and height and general color scheme can modify these requirements. A light color on the ceiling reflects 60 to 80 percent of the light; light reflection is reduced when dark colors are used; a kitchen with dark cabinets, counters, and/or walls needs to be equipped with more artificial light.

For sink-side tasks, provide 150 to 200 watts incandescent or 60 watts fluorescent. You can choose between recessing the lighting in, or mounting hanging fixtures from, the ceiling or soffit above the sink, mounting bullet fixtures on the wall or sides of adjacent wall cabinets, or mounting a 14- to 22-inch wall bracket.

The same treatment is recommended for over a range if there is no range hood, or if a hood is not equipped with lighting. A luminous back range panel adequately lights the controls, but is not sufficient light for the overall cooking surface.

For efficient counter illumination, allow one 20-watt fluorescent tube for every three feet of counter length, using a shielding device if tubes are mounted against the wall or in line of vision. In addition, if there is an eating area, plan a minimum of 150 watts incandescent light for dining.

ELECTRICAL OUTLETS

Your wiring plan should include: one 120-volt 15 ampere circuit for lights, clock, exhaust fan, and radio plus two 120-watt ampere circuits for small appliances. Also needed are separate—properly rated—circuits, for a refrigerator-freezer, dishwasher, disposer, electric range, or electric built-in oven and surface units. There should be one duplex outlet for every four feet of counter space, or convenient runway outlet strips.

If you are building or remodeling, it would be wise to check with your local utility company; most of them offer free analysis and recommendations for home lighting and wiring needs.

VENTILATION

Impurities in the air we breathe aren't confined just to the outside —the average home is saturated with airborne contaminants, and the biggest culprit is the kitchen. Unless removed, these impurities can cause numerous problems, and make more difficult the task of keeping the house and its furnishings clean.

VENTILATING FANS

The solution is an efficient, effective ventilating fan located as close as possible to the range, the primary source of many troublesome impurities—grease fumes, smoke, and water vapor. There are two basic types of ventilating fans; fans that are ducted to the outside (the most effective), and nonducted ones. Fans are usually installed within a range hood, built into a cabinet, or mounted in the wall or ceiling. To perform best, the bottom of the unit should be 27 to 30 inches above the cooking surface.

For safety, all ducted fans must be vented to the outside air— never into an attic. The ductwork can be vented directly through the wall, through the ceiling and roof, or through a concealed opening under the eaves. The shorter the length of ductwork, the higher the efficiency of the system will be—extra elbows drastically reduce the flow of air. Any changes in the size of the duct pipe should also be avoided, as this results in a waste of fan power.

When venting to the outdoors is not possible, you can use a ductless hood equipped with a fan and filter. These can trap odors as well as grease and smoke, and are a good solution for apartment dwellers or families who rent their home, or for those who live in an older home where the walls can't be remodeled.

In some cases, an exhaust fan may be the answer to keeping the air as healthy and the furnishings as clean as possible. These can be effective in removing smoke and cooking odors and to some extent help reduce heat and moisture in the kitchen. If mounted in a wall, the fan should be located directly behind and one to two feet above the range surface; if ceiling-mounted, it should be centered directly over the range.

CFM RATING

Ventilating and exhaust fans are rated according to the number of cubic feet of air they are capable of moving per minute. A change of air every four minutes is recommended for kitchens. By multiplying the number of square feet of the kitchen floor space by two, you can determine what CFM (cubic feet per minute) rating would be required to achieve this air exchange rate in your kitchen. (A kitchen with 90 square feet of room area would require a fan with a CFM rating of 180, for a change of air 15 times every hour.) If, however, your ceilings are higher than the average eight feet, you should get a fan with a slightly greater CFM rating. Often, code requirements set minimum CFM ratings for exhaust fans.

The wide-open plan that is prevalent in so many of today's homes makes proper ventilation a must if the atmosphere within the home is to remain healthy and comfortable, and the upkeep of walls and furnishings as carefree as possible. Here, a fan-equipped copper peninsula hood positioned over an island-contained indoor grill, meets ventilation requirements most attractively. Direct ducting to the outside through the ceiling permits the prompt removal of grease, smoke, odors, heat, and moisture. In addition, the hood itself extends beyond the perimeter of the grill and is so positioned that the bottom of the hood meets the recommendations—no more than 30 inches from the cooking surface—for optimum performance of the unit.

Incandescent bulbs located inside the hood provide the necessary—and most pleasing—type of light for eating as well as ample light to grill by.

chapter 9

MAINTENANCE AND SAFETY

Gone are the days when cleaning a kitchen was really drudgery. Thanks to modern technology, materials available today for cleaning floors, walls, countertops, and cabinets have considerably simplified the care of each. Now, kitchen upkeep requires only a minimum of effort.

Appliances, too, are easier than ever to maintain. Manufacturers have directed much effort in recent years toward engineering easy care into the design of their products. Seamless construction, rounded corners, lift-off doors, and lift-out components all speed up cleaning chores and save energy in the process.

Design engineers also have concentrated their efforts on building safety features into appliances. However, built-in safety measures can't supply the complete answer. It is up to the user to follow the instructions for the proper use of these appliances.

In addition, there are numerous other commonsense practices that will go a long way toward providing a safer environment in the kitchen and preventing needless accidents—accidents that could happen to you or to one of the members of your family.

Easy care is the byword for this well-planned kitchen. The floor, countertop, walls, and cabinets require little care. Good lighting contributes to safer working conditions. Work space separating the wall ovens and counter cook surface adds convenience.

MAINTENANCE

With proper care, floors, walls, appliances, and other surfaces of a kitchen stay new looking longer, and actually wear better.

Floors: Unless the floor covering is of the no-wax variety, washing and waxing are required. (Frequency depends upon the wear and tear the floor receives.) Some polishing waxes both clean and wax, but must be buffed (after application). Several waxings a year should be ample, with some patch waxing in between. Self-polishing waxes are easier to apply, but generally do not wear as long as polishing types. There are a few self-polishing types that can sustain several washings and can be reapplied a number of times before it is necessary to remove them. Two coats are better than one, and the floor can be damp-mopped between applications. Follow label instructions for removal of buildup.

Walls—painted or wallpapered: Paint and wallpaper, or wall covering used for kitchens, should be of the washable type. Wash in small sections, using a solution of detergent or a commercial cleaner and water. To prevent streaking, start at the top and wash down. If wallpaper is not washable, use wallpaper cleaner.

Windows: Clean with a commercial window cleaner or a solution of warm water and vinegar. One cleaning device cleans both sides of a window simultaneously. The outside unit holds magnetically to the master while you are cleaning the inside.

Counters—also cabinets of laminated plastic: Wipe often with a damp cloth; occasionally apply cream wax. Never use abrasives.

Wood cabinets: Follow manufacturer's recommendations or treat as you would fine furniture. Use either a wax or oily polish, but don't switch around. There are high- or low-luster types, depending on preference. Follow label directions. Waxes that dust and shine are quick and easy. If oily or sticky soils accumulate, use a cleaner wax that is designed for appliances.

Appliances: It's best to follow instructions in the use and care manual for each appliance. But, here are general care recommendations for the common finishes used for appliances.

1. Porcelain enamel. Wash with warm, sudsy water and rinse, or use a specially formulated appliance cleaner wax. To scour, use baking soda or a mild nonabrasive cleaner.

2. Baked enamel (also used for cabinets). Wash with warm, sudsy water, rinse. Wax cleaners can be used also. Acids damage; spray-on, wipe-off cleaners may dull the finish.

3. Acrylic enamel (also used for cabinets). Wash with sudsy water, rinse. Surface can be damaged by abrasive cleaners and all-purpose cleaners containing solvents.

4. Aluminum. Wash with hot sudsy water, or use steel wool.

5. Chromium. Wash with warm, sudsy water, polish dry. Do not use scouring pads, abrasives, or oven cleaners.

6. Stainless steel. Clean with solutions of detergent, ammonia, and water, polish dry. Cleaners with bleach will corrode finish.

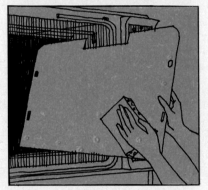

Lift-up range top

Removable oven liners

Magnetic window cleaning aid

Rollers for appliances

SAFETY

Numerous hazards prevail in a kitchen. Commonsense practices can avert accidents. Safety devices can be built into appliances, but product safety includes proper use and care.

Storage and use of cleaning supplies: Many of the household cleaners, bleaches, waxes, and cleaning fluids that we take for granted can be poisonous if swallowed or inhaled. When open, keep them under your watchful eye. Follow label directions for use. Provide good ventilation if suggested. Never transfer hazardous products into food-type containers. Store out of reach of youngsters, preferably under lock and key. If accidentally ingested or inhaled, take the container with you to the doctor so the poison can be identified and the proper treatment administered.

Be safety-minded with appliances: First, buy only those appliances that carry the UL symbol. Then, read the instruction booklets, and follow any specific safety procedures recommended for that particular appliance. They are suggested for your protection. Never let youngsters operate appliances. Make certain that all major appliances are grounded. Do not, however, ground appliances with open-coil heating elements—toasters and broilers. Never operate appliances close to the sink, and be sure that your hands are dry when using them. Use with the cord made for that particular appliance. Connect appliances to convenience outlets, not to extension cords. Have the wall outlets changed instead of removing the grounding wire of a three-prong plug.

Know the capacities of your circuits: Be familiar with wattages of appliances to avoid plugging more than 1600 watts into a general-purpose circuit, unless it is capable of handling more. A good rule of thumb is to connect no more than two motor-driven appliances or one heating appliance on the same circuit at the same time. Disconnect appliances when not in use, or before cleaning or oiling them. Grasp by the plug, not the cord. Remove first from the wall outlet, then remove from the appliance.

Keep appliances repaired: Don't fix them yourself unless you really know how. Replace loose plugs and worn cords.

GENERAL KITCHEN SAFETY-FIRST TACTICS

Wear well-fitting, tailored garments and low-heeled shoes for kitchen duty. Keep work surfaces uncluttered when preparing meals. Wipe up floor spills promptly. Keep cabinet doors and drawers closed when not in use. Have a sturdy stepladder handy.

Use the proper opener for bottles and containers—never a knife. Keep knives sharp, so strong pressure is not necessary. Store in a slotted tray or rack—never leave in a dishpan or under water.

Use common sense around the range. Use well-balanced, flat-bottomed cookware. Check handles to be certain they are attached well. Keep handles of pans turned inward. Keep baking soda, or a multipurpose, UL-approved fire extinguisher handy for any fire.

Fire extinguisher

Knobs out of children's reach

Hot pads and mitts

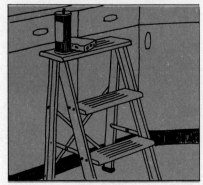
Stepladder

INDEX

ACKNOWLEDGMENTS FOR PHOTOGRAPHS

Androck Company
Arabesque, Div. of Burwood Products Co.
Arnoldware-Rodgers
Cheinco Housewares
Corning Glass Works
Grayline Housewares, Inc.
Mactac Div., Morgan Adhesives Co.
Magna Products Company
Martech, Inc.
Mutschler Kitchens
Omni Div., Hoover Ball and Bearing Co.
Parkwood Mobile Homes
Harper J. Ransburg, Inc.
Republic Molding Corporation
Sears Roebuck and Co.
Seth Thomas
Texas Ware Div., Plastics Mfg. Co.
Window Shade Manufacturers Assoc.